FINANCE FOR MANAGERS

CW01081838

FINANCE FOR MANAGERS

R. Vause and N. Woodward

First edition (under the title of
Finance for Non-Financial Managers) 1975
Second edition (under the present title) 1981

Published by
THE MACMILLAN PRESS LTD
London and Basingstoke
Companies and representatives
throughout the world

ISBN 0 333 308107 (hardcover)
ISBN 0 333 30651 1 (paperback)

Typeset in Great Britain by
STYLESET LIMITED
Salisbury, Wilts
and printed in Hong Kong

To Norman Leyland

The accountant wanted to be captain of the team, but they would not even let him play, giving him the job of scorer. So, in revenge, the accountant developed a system of scoring that no one else could understand.

Contents

Preface

Among the flurry of action within the accounting profession since the publication of our *Finance for Non-Financial Managers*, most notable has been the attempt to deal with inflation accounting. In this completely rewritten, retitled edition, a separate Chapter (4) is devoted to this topic, while the accounting profession's various Exposure Drafts and Standard Statements are listed in Chapter 1.

However, these changes have in no way diminished the need for a simple, clear introduction to finance and accounting for the layman, written for a managerial viewpoint. In this respect our objectives in writing this edition have not changed. For no manager can long avoid the need to understand a financial report, whether it be competitor's Balance Sheet, investment proposal, product cost sheet, or budgetary control report highlighting variances for the month. This book is written to provide the reader with a grasp of financial and management accounting and allied subjects sufficient to assess and use the accounting information available to him and to recognise where and how such information is relevant to his decisions.

Our emphasis throughout is upon clarity, simplicity and sense. If a manager, after reading this book is able to communicate confidently with his accountant, financial adviser, and anyone else who deals in accounting figures — if he can use their services, without being blinded by their figures — then this book will have succeeded in its intentions.

Oxford and London   R.V.
November 1979   N.W.

1 Introduction to Financial Accounting

For a proper appreciation of the various financial statements which companies and other organisations produce, a manager should have at least some understanding of the mechanics of financial accounting. This chapter explains the concepts, rules and assumptions used by financial accountants in the preparation and presentation of financial information for shareholders and other parties interested in the organisation's performance and financial situation. The concepts are, in themselves, straightforward and easy to grasp. The problems lie in their interpretation and application.

These concepts are important, because their impact on the understanding and interpretation of financial reports is great. For example, how can a business show a healthy profit in its annual accounts, but go into liquidation soon after? This occurrence can be explained by reference to one of the basic accounting concepts – accrual, discussed later in this chapter. Another question of frequent concern is how the balance sheet actually balances; yet the mechanics of double-entry book-keeping are based on a simple logical system.

It is not only managers who are concerned with financial statements such as the Profit and Loss Account and Balance Sheet of a company. A company's annual accounts are prepared primarily for the shareholders, a group one would expect to be able to understand such information. But this does not appear to be the case. In 1975 Lee and Tweedie[1] published the results of research into the nature and extent of users' understanding of company financial reports. The research concentrated on the private shareholder, not on institutional shareholders such as insurance companies who have a high degree of professional expertise in financial analysis. One of the conclusions was that the shareholder tended to be overconfident as to his or her ability to understand financial statements, and that 'an alarming degree of misunderstanding and ignorance of reporting practice has been evidenced amongst these private shareholders'. However, the private shareholder or manager need not feel too despondent. The same research study also showed that those within the survey group who had experience or education in finance or accounting showed no significantly better understanding of financial statements. When the reader has assimilated the initial chapters of this book he or she should be equipped to understand and interpret company reports.

There are two distinct types of accounting function that the manager will meet in the course of his work. The financial accountant is primarily concerned with the record-keeping aspect of company affairs, with the presentation of financial results to management, and with assisting in the assessment of the financial implications of management's decisions and policies. The financial accountant is also involved with the auditor in attempting to provide 'a clear and objective' view of the financial situation of the company for anyone who has the right to see it. In particular, they work together to prepare and present the accounts, the Annual Report containing the Profit and Loss Account for the year, and the Balance Sheet at the end of the year. The financial accountant will usually be a member of a professional body, such as the Institute of Chartered Accountants in England and Wales (ICA), and works within the boundaries defined by this body, within its rules, regulations, recommendations and ethical code, as well as having regard to the relevant legislation applying to companies and their financial reports – in particular the 1948, 1967 and 1976 Companies Acts. The manner in which professional bodies guide and control their members' work is discussed later in this chapter when the role of the auditor is considered.

The second type of accountant is the management accountant, who is often a member of The Institute of Cost and Management Accountants (ICMA). His main function is to assist management in decision- and policy-making activities. The management accountant provides managers in the organisation with accounting information relevant to their needs and responsibilities in planning and controlling operations. This information will rarely become public property, and the management accountant, although using the same framework as the financial accountant, is not subject to the same legal constraints in presenting data and information that pertain to formal public reporting of company performance. However, where the management accountant is a member of a professional body he will be expected to maintain the appropriate professional standards in his work. For example in March 1979 the ICMA produced detailed guidelines on the ethical standards expected of its members.[2] In general the management accountant tends to be concerned with the future, using data on the past to indicate trends, and to provide information for decisions on a firm's future direction and control. The financial accountant is often primarily concerned with the reporting of historic performance.

An apocryphal story will illustrate the difference between the two types of accountants. A managing director advertised for an accountant. He had conducted a great number of interviews and had developed interviewing to its ultimate skill. He asked each candidate the same question. There were three candidates who had the necessary qualifications and experience, and each was asked the single question, 'What is one and one?'. The first candidate, clearly a sound financial accountant, quickly replied, 'Two'. The second candidate was a bit smarter, and replied, 'It could be two, or it could be eleven'. The third, an experienced management accountant, answered, 'What are you doing, buying or selling?', and got the job.

The work of the management accountant and the nature of management accounting are discussed later. It is the work of the financial accountant that is considered in this chapter. The first step is to appreciate the fundamental concepts and conventions of financial accounting, together with the rules and guidelines which currently apply to the presentation of financial statements by companies.

1.1 ACCOUNTING CONCEPTS

(a) Business entity concept
In preparing a set of accounts for a company, the financial accountant uses the same assumption as the legal profession, that the limited company has a separate identity from the people that make the company function — the managers, directors, shareholders and other employees. This is termed the 'business entity concept'. The continued legal existence of a company is accordingly not affected by the death or dismissal of one of its directors. Although a 'one-man' company might be forced to cease trading on the death of its principal, the company would still exist as a legal entity, the shares being part of the estate. A limited company is assumed to have a 'corporate personality' and to have of itself rights and obligations independent of those who work in the company. A company may sue and be sued in its own name, and can enter into a binding contract with employees, as when the directors have service contracts with a company.

Even when a company is owned and run by the same people, the business entity concept holds good. One of the earlier cases on this subject was *Salomon* v. *Salomon & Co. Ltd* (1897), where it was held that the company must be treated as a separate identity even when the major shareholder is also a key director. The result of this ruling was that the director who had made a secured loan on the company could still rank preferentially (be paid out before) to the other creditors of the company, even though that director held the majority of the company's shares.

It may be thought that the business entity concept has little to do with financial accounting beyond defining the legal corporate identity. But it has a direct impact on the presentation of accounting information in annual

Balance Sheet.

Profit
+
Share
Capital =
Liability

reports. Indeed, it is this very concept that can be responsible for many of the problems managers have in reading accounts, particularly the Balance Sheet. It is this concept that necessitates any ploughed-back, or retained, profit to be shown as a liability in the Balance Sheet. This is because the 'company' owes to its shareholders the profit they have allowed it to retain, in just the same way as the 'company' owes them their original share capital.

Perhaps the most straightforward demonstration of the concept is to consider what happens when a company is wound up. The company cannot retain any funds when it ceases to exist, these funds must be distributed. The company realises its assets by selling them for cash, and then distributes (pays out) this cash to its creditors (people to whom the company owes money for goods and services provided), and repays any loans made to it by banks or other institutions or individuals. Finally, the company gives the balance of money remaining, if there is any, to the shareholders. The form of presentation of accounts of a company often reflects this process by the order in which the various groups of assets and liabilities of the company are set out in the Balance Sheet.

(b) Going concern concept

In preparing a set of accounts for a company the accountant assumes that the business is going to continue in existence for the foreseeable future, and that the business is not about to be sold or otherwise drastically altered. The accountant, in other words, assumes that there will be another set of accounts prepared for the company next year, and that this year's accounts are but one set in a long-continuing stream of such year-end reports. The going concern concept assumes that the company will continue in existence.

It is a common mistake to believe that the annual accounts show the value of the company at the year end. This is not the case, because the accountant, adopting the going concern concept, assumes, unless he has definite reasons to believe otherwise, that the company is going to continue trading in future years. The accountant is not preparing the accounts to show the value of the company at the year end if it were to be sold or liquidated (wound up).

However, if the auditor of a company has any reason to doubt the validity of applying the going concern concept to a company, then he must draw attention to this fact in the annual accounts in the Auditor's Report. An example of such situations can be seen in the 1978 Accounts of British Leyland (BL Ltd, 31 December 1978) where the auditors state that only if 'adequate finance will be available to meet the expenditure envisaged for the Company's plans' can the company be assumed to meet the requirements for the use of the going concern concept. Another example can be seen in the case of I.D. & S. Rivlin Holdings Ltd (30 April

1978) where the auditors in their report draw attention to the fact that the accounts are prepared on a going concern basis, but that this assumes continued bank overdraft facilities will be made available to the group to meet its needs in the future.

(c) Monetary quantification concept

Money is the common denominator of all business activity, and therefore the accountant prepares the accounts in the currency of the country relevant for his reporting purposes. It is axiomatic that a transaction or event cannot be translated into accounting terms unless it is capable of monetary quantification. If it is impossible to translate an event or transaction into monetary terms, the accountant cannot bring it into the accounts. The accountant is dealing with money transactions of the company, and with the assets (things which are of value and owned by the company) and liabilities (things that the company owes), and all are defined in monetary terms for inclusion in the Profit and Loss Account or Balance Sheet.

Though the adoption of the monetary quantification concept may seem commonsense and simple to operate, it creates several problems both for the accountant and for those who must interpret his figures. If valuation of the company is made on the sole basis of information in the Balance Sheet several factors will be disregarded which are of the utmost value to the firm (and thus affect its valuation), but which cannot be accurately translated into money terms. For example, the management team of a company with experience, expertise and ability never appear as an asset (or a liability) in the accounts. The 'cost' of the management team can easily be shown in the Profit and Loss Account under salaries, but it is difficult to envisage a practical and generally acceptable means of 'valuing' them for Balance Sheet purposes. There have been some attempts to value such assets – Human Asset Accounting[3] – but there is still some way to go before it can gain real practical acceptance by companies. Similarly, the firm's market strengths and market potential are not shown, except by means of past sales figures.

Part of this market standing is an asset whose value is difficult to quantify – the trade name. In the annual accounts of Marks & Spencer Ltd there is a comprehensive listing of assets and liabilities on 31 March each year, but nowhere is a figure placed on the value of the trade name 'St Michael'. But there can be no doubt that this is a valuable asset. Were another company to buy sole rights to its use, the cost of acquiring the trade name would be shown in the Profit and Loss Account, but an attempt to value 'St Michael' each year would prove difficult except on a very subjective basis. So it would be ignored once the purchase cost had been written off (charged in the Profit and Loss Account of the company).

6

Valuation of real but intangible assets is but one of the difficulties that stems from adoption of the monetary quantification concept. With a zero or low rate of inflation it is reasonable for the accountant to assume that a unit of currency at the beginning of the year is of the same value as one at the end of the year and to bring them together in both the Profit and Loss Account and the Balance Sheet. But with high levels of inflation the accountant is left with a monetary unit, which is the common denominator of business, but elastic and no longer stable from month to month. Some possible solutions to this problem are considered separately in connection with Current Cost Accounting (CCA) or 'inflation accounting' in Chapter 4.

There will be occasions when the accountant cannot accurately place a monetary value on an item which is relevant to the assessment of a company's financial position. Take, for instance, the 1977 Accounts of Bryant Holdings Ltd, a building and engineering group which was committed for trial on charges of corruption between 1963–73. At the end of the company's financial year (31 May 1977) the outcome of the trial was unknown, so it was impossible to quantify for accounting purposes the liability the company might incur if the case were proved. Yet in assessing the company's financial position it was important to draw attention to this possible liability. This was done in the notes on the accounts headed 'contingent liability' in the 1977 Annual Report, and mentioned in the auditor's report. Thus anyone reading the accounts of the company had information provided to enable them to interpret the financial statements.

(d) Realisation concept

Practising managers often find the financial accountant rather negative in his approach to business problems. Accountants are indeed circumspect in what they accept for accounting purposes. For instance, revenue from a sale will not be accepted in the Profit and Loss Account until the sale has been finally completed with ownership of the goods or services legally passing to the customer. This is an example of the realisation concept. The term 'realisation' here means that for a sale, goods must have been provided and cash received, or a clear legal obligation created for the customer to pay in the future. Until this is the case the accountant will not show the income in the Profit and Loss Account.

If in November a company manufactures a batch of its products to a customer's order, and delivers them to the customer in December, the revenue, or sale, is not deemed to have taken place, as far as the accountant is concerned, until December. The mere manufacture of items against a customer's order does not in itself count as a sale, so if the company were to draw up its accounts in November the goods concerned would appear in stock (valued at cost), and not revenue (including the profit on the goods). If, however, the accounts are drawn up for December, then the goods will be shown as part of the company's revenue in the Profit and Loss Account whether or not cash has been received.

Where a company revalues assets to bring them into line with current asset values the increase in value will not be shown as a profit. This is because the gain will not be 'realised' until the assets are sold, and only at this stage will it be included in the Profit and Loss Account of the company. Even then this increase in the value of assets will be shown separately, to distinguish it from the normal trading or operating profit of the business. It will be shown in a separate reserve in the Balance Sheet as part of the Shareholders' interest.

(e) Accrual concept

Under the realisation concept it was stated that once a sale has legally taken place, whether or not cash has been received from the customer for the goods delivered, the transaction will be taken as a sale, and included as part of the sale revenue appearing in the Profit and Loss Account. This illustrates the operation of the accrual concept.

It is this concept that can account for the fact that a company showing a good profitability in its Profit and Loss Account can go bankrupt soon after the accounts are produced. Accountants are not interested only in the cash movement in the firm. In preparing a Profit and Loss Account the accountant is trying to measure for a given time period – normally one year – the revenues and expenses of the business. It does not matter, for the purposes of accounting in the Profit and Loss Account, whether or not the revenues or the expenses have been received in cash or paid.

Suppose a company purchases materials from a supplier and then, using those materials, sells the finished product to a customer. Even if the company has not yet settled the supplier's bill, these materials will be shown in the Profit and Loss Account as a cost against the revenue generated. In the same manner, if the customer has not yet paid cash for the products he has received, this will still be shown as a part of the sales revenue figure appearing in the Profit and Loss Account.

It is thus possible in the short term for there to be little relationship between profitability and the cash generated by a company. A company which buys materials on credit and sells on credit can find itself in a cash crisis if the credit it extends to its customers is longer than credit allowed it by its suppliers. The Profit and Loss Account may show a very sound profitability, but there may be no cash in the bank to pay the coming week's wage bill, or a supplier demanding immediate payment. Where a company has a large proportion of its sales to a single customer, it is particularly vulnerable to that customer's financial health, apart from any considerations of marketing strategy.

(f) Valuation concept

Until the last few years accountants, when valuing assets for inclusion in the Balance Sheet of a company, used historic cost as the basis for such valuations. This cost is the actual cost to the company at time of purchase (with depreciation based on this). The main attraction for the cost basis of valuation is that the cost of an asset is the only valuation which it is impossible to dispute. And since, under the 'going concern' concept, the Balance Sheet is not an attempt to value the company in terms of what the assets could be sold for, under conditions of low inflation valuation at historic cost proved perfectly adequate for most purposes.

However, with the rapid inflation of the past few years, using historic cost as the sole basis for asset valuation has proved ineffective and often misleading. For the assets of the company become 'undervalued' and the amount set aside in the Profit and Loss Account for depreciation is inadequate. The reason is that the current (or replacement) cost of an asset now is typically much greater under inflation than its historic purchase cost. The use of historic cost, with depreciation based on this, ignores this inflation in the asset's price. Substantial inflation in property values has led many companies to revalue these in their Balance Sheets, so as to provide a better indication of the real investment and capital employed in the business. However, the way in which this is done, and how the values are reported has been so far left very much to the discretion of the directors of the company, with few formal or standard guidelines to assist in the process.

In brief, in the last ten years the well-established use of historic cost as a basis for valuation has proved ineffective for financial reporting, so Historic Cost Accounting (HCA) is giving place to Current Cost Accounting (CCA) as the accounting profession faces the challenge of maintaining the credibility of the financial statements it produces. The development and mechanics of CCA, and of the problems of inflation accounting are discussed in Chapter 4.

(g) Consistency concept

Accountants often come under criticism for an apparent unwillingness to change their treatment and presentation of financial information. The reason for this consistency of approach is important, and reinforced by strict training. If accountants were not consistent in their treatment of the various expenses, revenues, assets and liabilities of the company, it would create chaos for those trying to interpret and analyse company accounts. If each year the method of valuing a company's stock were changed, comparison through the years of the performance of that company would be difficult, since profitability as well as the assets would change as a result of the alteration in stock values. There would be no common basis for the analysis of its financial reports and each analyst would have to try to rework the accounts to a comparable annual basis. This is why accountants are very reluctant to change their treatment of the various items incorporated into the annual accounts of a company. If they do change, then there will be notification of the change by way of a note in accounts. Even as it is, in comparing results between companies, one has to ensure that differences in reporting conventions are taken into account.

(h) Prudence concept

Financial accountants are often seen, as a professional body, to be ultra-conservative or, less diplomatically, pessimistic, in their approach to corporate reporting, an image which provides grounds for caricature in the media (see Fig. 1.1). Part of the reason for this perception has been explained in the previous sections dealing with basic accounting concepts. Take for example the way in which the financial accountant values inventory at either cost or net realisable value, whichever is the lower, at the Balance Sheet date. When net realisable value is higher than cost (the company could sell it for more than it cost) the accountant ignores the unrealised gain. When net realisable value is lower than cost, this figure is used in the Accounts even though the 'loss' has not been realised. To an entrepreneurial manager, whose stock-in-trade is the ability to realise apparently unjustified confidence, and sell his optimism to bankers, customers, commentators and investors, this professional prudence must seem like obstructive conservatism, making his job doubly difficult.

But the financial accountant must exercise caution in order to avoid misleading those reading his figures. The auditor signs the annual accounts of a company as showing a 'true and fair view of the state of affairs'. He must be careful in the extreme, since others may take action on the basis of the information contained in the accounts. If the accountant were to mislead (particularly on the side of optimism) on a company's situation, he might be open to legal action by anyone acting on the information in his accounts, as well as professional criticism for his actions. From management's point of view it can be a nuisance to have an accountant who wishes to verify their actions and activities, and to keep comprehensive records, but in this work the accountant is providing safeguards for all those interested in the company's affairs. Not even an exotic bottle of vodka can transfigure this need for professional prudence.

(i) Materiality concept

One of the principal duties of the financial accountant is to maintain a careful record of the various transactions of a company, and of its assets and liabilities. This requirement was reinforced by the 1976 Companies Act. Such records must be retained for a number of years by the company

Fig. 1.1

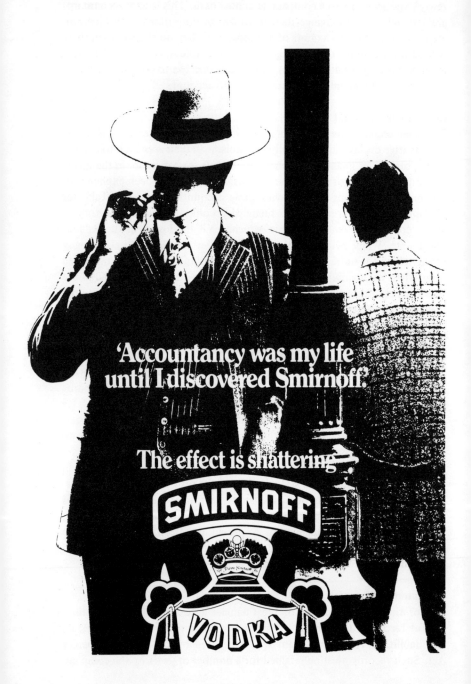

(three years for a private company and six years for a public company). But there are, of necessity, limits beyond which the accountant need not go. There would be little sympathy for the accountant who measured the length of unused pencils in the company offices so as to record these as an asset at the year-end. Not only would such a course of action be impracticable, but it would be of little value in analysing that company's performance or financial stability.

The accountant's concern is with material fact, and he should produce only relevant information. With the unused pencils, the accountant would probably treat the total amount of pencils purchased, (possibly after an adjustment for opening and closing stock changes), as an expense in the Profit and Loss Account, without further analysis. The accountant can adopt a simple test for materiality. If leaving the item out could possibly mislead a reader of the accounts as to the performance or financial position of the company, then it should be included in the accounts.

1.2 DUTIES OF ACCOUNTANTS – THE AUDITOR

The financial accountant who produces information for presentation in an organisation's annual accounts or other financial statements is expected to be free from bias and completely objective in his work. To a large extent this is guaranteed by application of the basic accounting concepts discussed above, but it is worth emphasising, as it is vital to the appreciation of financial reports. Information presented by the financial accountant should be capable of independent verification. It is the professional auditor who is expected to undertake the task of verifying the information presented in the annual accounts.

The auditor, the professional financial accountant who will sign the company's accounts as being a good representation of the state of affairs, is employed by the shareholders of the company. He is not employed by the directors of the company, except where the directors happen also to be major shareholders of the company. The auditor's duties are closely defined both by statute and case law, as well as by the professional code of the institute of which he is a member.

The auditor prepares his report for the shareholders and as the shareholders cannot themselves be expected to check the records of the company, he undertakes this task for them. To enable the auditor to carry out his responsibilities fully, he is to some extent protected from management pressure by the fact that he cannot be summarily dismissed by the directors without being offered the right to put his case to the shareholders concerning the conflict between the directors and himself.

The exact duties of the auditor are often misunderstood, which can lead to a false sense of security when looking at a set of accounts signed by a professional firm of accountants. While the auditor is expected to use his professional skills to the full and to follow the various rules and regulations relating to company accounts, he is basically concerned with the record-keeping of the company. Does the Profit and Loss Account adequately show the revenues and expenses of the company for the period covered? Are the assets and liabilities correctly listed in the Balance Sheet in a manner which meets his professional approval? To ensure that this is the case, the auditor must collect sufficient information, and check it for accuracy, to enable him to present his findings to the shareholders in the required manner.

There is no requirement that the auditor prepare the necessary data to produce the annual accounts of an organisation. This is the responsibility of the organisation's own accountants. The auditor's job is to check the adequacy and accuracy of the internal record-keeping. Should the auditor not be satisfied, then he will draw attention to the deficiencies in the organisation's internal accounts in the auditor's report which is attached to the annual accounts.

The auditor is not required to comment on the management of the company unless it directly relates to the presentation of the information to the shareholders in the Annual Report. A case where the auditor could be expected to make comment is where he finds that the company has not been maintaining adequate records of its trading, which makes it difficult to ensure the accuracy of the Profit and Loss Account or the amounts owed to or by the company.

The auditor is not expected to give advice to the management of the company in the running of their business. He may offer advice on the accounting system operated by the company, but even here there is no statutory obligation on him to do so.

The discovery and prevention of fraud is often taken to be a prime objective of the auditor. But this is not the case. The auditor has no direct responsibility for this. Fraud is a matter for the management and accountants employed by the company. The 1976 Companies Act strengthened the position of the auditor by making it a criminal offence to mislead him. In the *Kingston Cotton Mills* case (1896) the auditor was described by Lopes L. J. as a 'watchdog, but not a bloodhound'. Once the auditor has found something wrong with the accounting records of an organisation he must notify the directors at once and undertake detailed examination of relevant parts of the accounting system to discover the extent of the problem.[4]

The auditor is mainly concerned with the presentation of financial information in the legally defined manner to shareholders of the company. However, the majority of auditors who are professionally trained, competent accountants do take their duties beyond the required minimum, and offer assistance to management. Many of the larger firms of professional accountants offer (through separate departments) a range of management services and consultancy advice.

It is not currently possible to state the limit of auditor's liability for the use made of an organisation's accounts once he has signed them. The case of *Chandler* v. *Crane Christmas & Co* (1951) indicated that, as far as the law is concerned, the auditor has no duty to third parties who use his signed accounts. But *Hedley Byrne & Co. Ltd.* v. *Heller and Partners Ltd* (1963), though not dealing directly with accounting matters, did have a bearing on the position of auditors. The Hedley Byrne case suggested that accountants preparing and signing accounts could find themselves liable to third parties who act upon the strength of their information. The Institute of Chartered Accounts consulted Counsel on the implications of this case for their members and the opinion was given that an auditor would be unlikely to incur liability to a third party who took investment decisions on the basis of a set of accounts prepared in the normal course of corporate reporting. However, auditing firms in America have been successfully sued over negligent work, and such experience casts some doubt on the current position of UK auditors in this respect.

By law, an auditor must be a member of a professional body, and in recent years attention has been paid to the way in which the professional bodies control their members and enforce at least the minimum acceptable standards of performance. The Institute of Chartered Accountants has a Disciplinary Committee to which members may be reported for unprofessional conduct, and the Institute's monthly journal *Accountancy* publishes a report of the Committee's findings. The Institute also has a detailed Ethical Guide for members. The Professional Standards Committee (PSC) was set up in 1976 to improve overall professional standards of members and to consider the validity of specific criticisms of members' work.

The Auditing Practices Committee (APC) keeps auditors up to date on current issues and problems in auditing work. The Union Européenne des Experts Comptables Economiques et Financiers (UEC) has an Auditing Statements Board (ASB) which produces definitive statements dealing with auditing matters. For example their Auditing Statement number 4 (1978) dealt with the auditing implications of preparing accounts on a going concern basis (see Section 1.1(b)). The ASB's objectives are to:

(i) raise the standard of auditing in Europe;
(ii) harmonise the audit of financial statements;
(iii) promote the development of auditing principles and techniques;
(iv) improve the mutual understanding of auditor's reports on financial statements of business enterprises.

The International Federation of Accountants (IFA) has an International Auditing Practices Committee (IAPC), and the Consultative Committee of Accountancy Bodies (CCAB) develops Statements for the guidance of members of the UK professional bodies. The first Statement (1979) dealt with professional independence of accountants to ensure that high standards of professional integrity and objectivity are maintained (see Section 1.1(h)).

In 1976 the Cross Committee, under the chairmanship of Lord Cross, was set up to consider the need and practicability of overseeing the level of professional competence of members of the main professional accountancy bodies. In 1978 the Grenside Report was published, suggesting practical means of achieving this. The recommendations of the Grenside Report include the setting up of a Practice Advisory Service for accountants, and a concentration on continuing professional education of members as aids to self-discipline by the profession.

This activity was stimulated by a series of public criticisms of specific work undertaken by professional accountants and Department of Trade (DOT) Reports on certain companies' financial affairs. Indeed there have been proposals that the DOT should take control of the accounting profession and enforce the necessary standards. The Labour Economic Finance and Taxation Association (LEFTA) published a pamphlet[5] putting forward strong recommendations in this respect.

The accountancy profession has attempted to maintain its independence by putting its own house in order and exercising firm discipline on professional standards and the activities of accountants, in particular with the above-mentioned committees whose job it is to oversee professional work by accountants.

Finally, the idea has been mooted of forming company-based Audit Committees to assist auditors in their work. An Audit Committee would consist of non-executive directors of the company and representatives of the auditors, and would offer an opportunity for improving communication between auditors and the main Board of the Company.[6]

1.3 ACCOUNTING STANDARDS

To provide better standardisation of the treatment and presentation of financial information in published statements specific guidelines are published by the relevant bodies in different countries. The USA has the Financial Accounting Standards Board (FASB), and in the UK there is the Accounting Standards Steering Committee (ASSC). The ASSC publishes an Exposure Draft (ED) on a particular subject for comment and discussion, and then a Statement of Standard Accounting Practice (SSAP) with which professional financial accountants are expected to comply.

When the first edition of this book was completed in 1974 three SSAPs had been published and ED number 8 (on inflation accounting) was being discussed. By May 1979 fifteen SSAPs had been published, and ED number 24 had just been issued, dealing with current cost accounting (inflation accounting). This illustrates the recent concern in the accounting bodies for standardisation of accounting practice, as well as the problems encountered in reaching positive conclusions on how to treat inflation in financial reporting.

The Accounting Standards Committee is made up of representatives from the major UK accounting bodies: The Institute of Chartered Accountants in England and Wales, The Institute of Chartered Accountants of Scotland, The Institute of Chartered Accountants in Ireland, The Association of Certified Accountants, The Institute of Cost and Management Accountants, and the Chartered Institute of Public Finance and Accountancy.

The subjects upon which SSAPs have been issued are as follows:

SSAP 1 (1971) Accounting for the results of associated companies;
2 (1971) Disclosure of accounting policies;
3 (1972) Earnings per share;
4 (1974) The accounting treatment of government grants;
5 (1974) Accounting for value added tax;
6 (1974) Extraordinary items and prior year adjustments;
8 (1974) The treatment of taxation under the imputation system;
9 (1975) Stocks and work in progress;
10 (1975) Statements of sources and application of funds;
12 (1977) Accounting for depreciation;
13 (1977) Accounting for research and development;
14 (1978) Group Accounts;
15 (1978) Accounting for deferred taxation.
16 (1980) Current Cost Accounting.

SSAP 7 (1974) dealt with inflation accounting, and SSAP 11 (1975) with deferred taxation, but both have now been superseded.

While it is not relevant to go into the detail of the various SSAPs, managers may need to consult them on particular issues, and reference will be made to them in later chapters. Appendix 1 lists the plethora of acronyms prevalent in accounting literature.

2 Financial Reporting

In the first chapter the basic concepts underlying financial accounting were presented. This chapter shows how the financial statements that organisations publish each year are built up and presented.

The basic reporting period that accountants use is the calendar year of twelve months. The date upon which the annual accounts of an organisation are drawn up signifies that year's end. Breaking down financial reporting into annual lumps can have drawbacks if it does not reflect sales or other cycles and there is little evidence to suggest that this arbitrary time period gives the best information as to the real development of an organisation. Implementation of technology, exploitation of markets, training of personnel may take a longer or shorter period depending on the industry. But in most countries it is the law that demands that companies prepare at least annual accounts. This is often for tax reasons, as well as to safeguard the shareholders' interests by not letting too long a period elapse between performance by the company and the reporting of that performance.

The 1948 and 1976 Companies Acts require companies to maintain 'adequate' financial records. Many managers are put off by the apparently complicated and mysterious system of book-keeping that accountants use, and shy away from financial reports. This chapter provides the basic information for understanding such reports, for it is pointless to attempt analysis of an accounting report unless the manner in which a set of accounts is prepared has been understood. To achieve this the manager need not become a trained accountant. The illustrations in this chapter are simple, and will not enable the manager either to maintain a set of accounting records or to prepare his own accounts. Anyone requiring this competence should consult some of the numerous books available on basic accounting or book-keeping.

2.1 THE MECHANICS OF BASIC ACCOUNTING – DOUBLE-ENTRY BOOK-KEEPING

Double-entry book-keeping appears to have been 'invented' towards the beginning of the fourteenth century. The name most often associated with it at this period is that of Paccioli, who wrote on the subject of record-keeping in Italy and, as an itinerant mathematics teacher, also devoted some time to gambling and probability analysis.

The basic concept of double-entry book-keeping is extremely simple. It is that *every recorded transaction shall have two entries in the books of account.*

To illustrate the process of double-entry book-keeping in connection with the preparation of a set of annual accounts, assume that two brothers, John and Ben, decide to set up a small company to manufacture a product John has invented. Between them they have £5,000 with which to start the venture. Having formed a limited company, their first action is to open a bank account for the company, and to pay into it the £5,000. The company is now in existence and must maintain records of its transactions. Working from the Cash Account of the company, the first entry would be:

CASH ACCOUNT

1 Jan. Capital introduced   £5,000 |

What has to be done is to enter on the left-hand side of the page which is to record the company's cash transactions the fact that £5,000 has been paid into the account to start the business. However, this is only a single entry, and to fulfil the requirement of double-entry book-keeping a further entry is required. This would be:

SHARE CAPITAL ACCOUNT

| 1 Jan. John and Ben, cash introduced £5,000

A second account has been opened to record the fact that John and Ben have provided the initial capital of the company. In the case of the second entry in the Share Capital Account, the figure has been placed on the opposite side of the page to the one appearing in the Cash Account. This reflects the simple rule that all cash coming into the business is shown on the left-hand side of the Cash Account, and cash going out will appear on the right-hand side of the Cash Account. This provides the basis for completing the other accounts in the records of the company.

The rule concerning two entries for each transaction can be restated as: whatever has been put on the left-hand side of an account, an equal sum must be entered on the right-hand side of another account. This has been followed in the two entries above: one on the left, and one on the right. The initial transaction, or movement of cash, to set the company up has been completed with the two entries in the books of account.

The next step for John and Ben is that they purchase for cash a machine with which to manufacture their product, and pay the first month's rent on the workshop they are to use. These transactions are recorded in the Cash Account as:

CASH ACCOUNT

1 Jan. Capital introduced	5,000	5 Jan. Machine purchased	3,600
		7 Jan. January rent paid	100

The second entry relating to each of these cash outflows for the company is as follows:

MACHINE ACCOUNT

5 Jan. Cash paid	3,600

RENT ACCOUNT

7 Jan. January rent paid	100

For each type of transaction a new account is opened and used to compile the double-entry book-keeping process. It can now be seen that if the mechanical process of book-keeping with double entry is maintained without error, at any stage of the year the books of the company will be in balance. Or, to put this another way, at any stage *the total of all entries on the left-hand side of all the accounts will equal the total of all entries on the right-hand side of all the accounts.* Thus, on 7 January the position is:

Left-hand side		*Right-hand side*	
Cash Account	5,000	Share Capital Account	5,000
Machine Account	3,600	Cash Account	3,700
Rent Account	100		
	£8,700		£8,700

The total of all entries on the left-hand side is £8,700, and this balances with the £8,700 appearing for the right-hand side entries. It is this fact that is at the heart of book-keeping and, as will be shown later, enables the Profit and Loss Account and Balance Sheet to be drawn up with a minimum of trouble.

The company, having installed the machine, next purchases some raw materials in order to manufacture a batch of the product ready for sale. A supplier agrees to deliver the raw materials on the understanding that his bill is settled within thirty days for the full amount of £800. The materials are delivered to the company's workshop and there now exists an obligation on the company to pay the supplier £800. The company has also obtained an asset – the raw materials which it can use in production. These two facts make up the two sides of the entries in the company's books:

RAW MATERIALS ACCOUNT

10 Jan.   Delivered by XYZ Ltd £800 |

CREDITORS ACCOUNT

| 10 Jan. XYZ Ltd   £800

Two new accounts have been opened: one to record the asset, raw materials; the other to record the obligation, or liability, that the company has incurred, to pay supplier XYZ Ltd for the goods delivered. When the company pays the supplier there will be two entries to record this fact. The one will be placed on the right-hand side of the Cash Account to record the payment of £800, and the other on the left-hand side of the Creditors Account to show that the company no longer owes the supplier any money.

A simple series of rules can be developed to show how any transaction a company undertakes should be recorded:

A.   Cash paid out and the obligation to pay out cash in the future are recorded on the right-hand side of the appropriate account.
B.   Cash paid in, and the increase in the assets owned by the company, are recorded on the left-hand side of the appropriate account.
C.   Expenses that the company incurs are entered on the left-hand side of the appropriate account.
D.   Revenues or other income that the company produces are entered on the right-hand side of the appropriate account.

If these four simple rules are checked against the entries made for John and Ben, they will be seen to have been followed throughout. Note that cash paid out is distinguished from expenses, and cash paid in distinguished from revenues.

Next, the company manufactures a batch of its product, and sells it to customers in the locality. All the raw materials from XYZ Ltd are used up in producing sales of £1,900. The Sales Account is shown below and, following Rule D given above, the revenue is shown on the right-hand side of the account:

SALES ACCOUNT

	20 Jan. To various customers	1,900

By the end of January the company has received £1,200 in cash from customers, and is still owed £700 from firms John and Ben are certain will pay within the following month — there are no bad debts likely. To record these debtors a new account is used; as debts owed to the company are an asset, the entry is placed on the left-hand side of the account. This is the reverse of what was done in the creation of the Creditors Account.

DEBTORS ACCOUNT

20 Jan. Various customers	£700	

The £1,200 that the company has received in cash for sales will have been entered into the left-hand side of the Cash Account. Thus, there is £1,900 appearing on the right-hand side of the Sales Account, and this is balanced by £1,200 on the left of the Cash Account, and £700 on the left of the Debtors Account.

If the transactions detailed above conclude the activity of the company in the first month of operations, it is possible to draw up a Profit and Loss Account and Balance Sheet to record the results. The first step in this will be to balance off each account. The Cash Account will now appear as:

CASH ACCOUNT

1 Jan. Capital introduced	5,000	5 Jan. Machine purchased	3,600
20 Jan. Sales to customers	1,200	7 Jan. January rent paid	100
		30 Jan. Heat and power paid	200
		31 Jan. Balance carried down	2,300
	£6,200		£6,200
31 Jan. Balance brought down	2,300		

There are two entries in the Cash Account that require further explanation. The payment for heat and power covers the first month of the company's operations in the workshop, and was paid over to the landlord on the last day of the month. A separate account will have been opened to record this transaction, an expense to the company. The balance that exists in the Cash Account is £2,300; this is the amount of cash that the company has on 31 January. To balance off the account on the last day of the month, this amount must be added to the right-hand side, and it is brought down in the account to start off the records for February; this is done, as can be seen, using two entries.

Cash is clearly an asset to the company, and the Cash Account illustrates an extension to the rules above. This can be expressed as two further rules:

E. Assets of the company will appear as balances on the left-hand side of accounts.
F. Liabilities of the company will appear as balances on the right-hand side of accounts.

2.2 THE PROFIT AND LOSS ACCOUNT

The first stage in drawing up a set of accounts is the drafting of the Profit and Loss Account for the period. This account deals with the revenue that has been generated during the period, and with the costs and expenses incurred in the generation of that revenue. The Profit and Loss Account can be regarded as a statement of the change in the shareholders' stake in the company during the period, since the final profit shown in the Profit and Loss Account represents the amount of increase in the shareholders' interest in the company. Throughout the production of the Profit and Loss Account the double-entry book-keeping procedure is maintained, but this time it is used to transfer items from their original account into the Profit and Loss Account. One entry is made in the original account, and the second, for the same amount, is made in the Profit and Loss Account. The completed Profit and Loss Account is shown below:

JOHN & BEN LTD

PROFIT AND LOSS ACCOUNT FOR JANUARY

(B) Raw materials consumed	800	(A) Sales		1,900
(C) Rent	100			
(D) Heat and power	200			
(E) Depreciation of machine	100			
(F) Profit for the month	700			
	£1,900			£1,900
		(F) Profit for month		700

To illustrate the process of preparing the Profit and Loss Account for entry (A) dealing with sales, the Sales Account would have had an entry made on the left-hand side:

| 31 Jan. | To Profit and Loss Account | £1,900 | 20 Jan. | To various customers | £1,900 |

This half of the double entry takes the sales revenue generated during the month out of the Sales Account; the other half entry **(A)** to the Profit and Loss Account brings sales into that account. The sales revenue for the month then has the expenses and cost set against it to determine whether a profit or loss has been made for the month. It will be noted that the total amount of sales is brought into the Profit and Loss Account, not just the £1,200 that has been received in cash by the end of the month. The Profit and Loss Account is dealing with revenues and expenses for a given time period, irrespective of whether they have been paid in cash at the time of the Profit and Loss Account's preparation.

Entry **(B)** in the Profit and Loss Account records the fact that £800 worth of raw materials has been used in the generation of the sales revenue. The same mechanical process would be followed to bring this amount into the account as was done with sales — except this time from the opposite side of the account because it is an expense, not revenue.

Entries **(C)** and **(D)** would be made in the same manner to bring the correct charge into the Profit and Loss Account.

Entry **(E)** deals with the recording of the depreciation of the machine. There should be an entry in the Profit and Loss Account to account for the use of the machine during the month, and to provide for its eventual replacement when it is worn out. Depreciation is discussed in more detail in Chapter 3, but for the moment let a simple means of depreciation be used. Assume that the expected life of the machine is three years; using this, it is possible to assess how much depreciation should be charged in the January Profit and Loss Account:

$$\frac{\text{Initial cost of the machine}}{\text{Estimated life of machine}} = \frac{£3,600}{36 \text{ months}} = £100 \text{ per month}$$

To record depreciation adequately a new account must be opened, and the details entered in conjunction with the Machine Account:

DEPRECIATION ACCOUNT

| 31 Jan. Machine depreciation | 100 | |

MACHINE ACCOUNT

5 Jan. Cash paid	3,600	31 Jan. January depreciation	100
		31 Jan. Balance carried down	3,500
	£3,600		£3,600
31 Jan. Balance brought down	3,500		

The Machine Account has had depreciation charged for the month, and this is deducted from the original cost by the entry of £100 on the right-hand side of the account. This charge is taken to the Depreciation Account to complete the two entries necessary to record the charge. Entry (E) is made to the Profit and Loss Account, completing that account.

Having entered all the revenues and expenses in the Profit and Loss Account, all that remains to be done is to balance the account off. This is done by entry (F), which is the balancing figure necessary to make both sides of the account equal each other (£700). This shows that revenue has exceeded cost by £700, so the company has made a profit for the month of January. The balancing figure is brought down in the account ready for transfer to the Balance Sheet.

2.3 THE BALANCE SHEET

The Balance Sheet of the company is set out below, and lists, as its name suggests, the balances existing on the books of the company on a certain day — in this case, 31 January. This is all the Balance Sheet is. It does not attempt to show the value of the company, but to state in book-keeping terms the assets and liabilities of the company on the Balance Sheet day.

JOHN & BEN LTD

BALANCE SHEET, 31 JANUARY

Share Capital	5,000	(d)	Machine	3,500	(a)
Profit and Loss Account	700	(e)	Debtors	700	(b)
Creditor XYZ Ltd	800	(f)	Cash	2,300	(c)
	£6,500			£6,500	

The left-hand side of the Balance Sheet lists the liabilities of the company on 31 January, and the right-hand side the assets on this date. If the double-entry book-keeping routine has been maintained correctly, it must balance.

To find the entries for the Balance Sheet, each account in the company's books is studied to see if it has a balance on it. If it has a balance on the right-hand side, then this is a liability (Rule F above); if on the left-hand side, this is an asset.

In the traditional UK Balance Sheet the liabilities are listed on the left-hand side, and assets on the right. This means that where a balance is on the left-hand side of an account, as with the Machine Account, then it is put on the right-hand side of the Balance Sheet – entry (*a*). This is a contradiction of the double-entry book-keeping rule by which a left-hand balance should appear on the left-hand side of the Balance Sheet. This method of reversing double entry at the Balance Sheet is peculiar to the UK.

Entries (*b*) and (*c*) are made in the same way as for the Machine Account, and when they are added together they provide the total for the right-hand side of the Balance Sheet (£6,500). If the books have been properly kept, it will be possible to find the remaining balances on the right-hand side of accounts that total the same amount.

The Share Capital Account shows a balance of £5,000 on the right-hand side, and this is entered on the left-hand side of the Balance Sheet as entry (*d*). This figure represents the amount that the company 'owes' to its shareholders. If the company were to go into liquidation, and the assets to achieve their stated values, this amount of £5,000 would be paid back to the shareholders; they would get their money back. As well as receiving their original capital back the shareholders would be entitled to the profit that the company has made. This is the balance on the Profit and Loss Account which is transferred to the Balance Sheet in entry (*c*).

The only remaining balance on the books of the company is the £800 appearing in the Creditors Account. This £800 is brought into the Balance Sheet by entry (*f*).

The accounts for John & Ben Ltd are now complete, and all the available information has been extracted from the company's record. Clearly, in real life the situation would be far more complex, with many more entries and accounts being made in the books of the company, but this simple example illustrates the process that the accountant goes through in maintaining records for a firm, and preparing the accounts.

The system of double-entry book-keeping has been explained without reference to the terms 'debit' and 'credit', which accountants commonly use in their work. These terms have been avoided because they do not assist the non-financial manager in understanding the mechanics of book-keeping. Indeed, they only confuse the issue.

All a debit means is that the entry is to be made on the left-hand side of the account. Thus, if the Cash Account is debited for £5,000, this means that £5,000 is written in the left-hand side of that account.

Credit means the opposite of debit. If an account is credited, then an entry is made on the right-hand side of that account. Debit and credit are purely locational terms for the accountant. They have no other significance. In double-entry book-keeping every transaction must have a debit and credit.

2.4 BALANCE SHEET PRESENTATION

In the following chapters of this book the basic pattern of accounting will be expanded and developed to provide a fuller understanding of real-life company accounts. But before this is done, the presentation of the annual accounts of companies must be considered. With very few exceptions, companies do not provide a left-hand and right-hand side Balance Sheet or Profit and Loss Account. They use the same process of book-keeping previously outlined, but in presenting their annual accounts it is ignored.

Fig. 2.1 *Balance sheet building blocks*

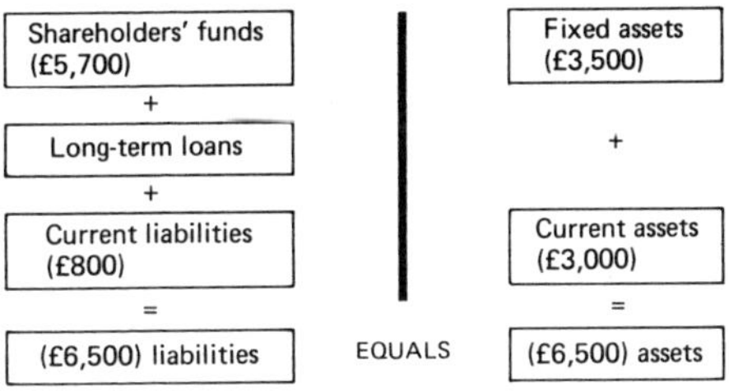

The basic building blocks of the Balance Sheet are shown in Fig. 2.1 for a traditional layout. The figures in brackets relate to the Balance Sheet of John & Ben Ltd, in Section 2.3. On the liabilities side of the Balance Sheet, there is the information on where the financing has come from, or what the company owes. The first block relates to the shareholders' interest in the company. The second block does not apply to John & Ben Ltd, and is for any long-term loans that the company has received. The third block is the current liabilities; these are the short-term liabilities of the company. In the case of John & Ben Ltd they consist of the money owed to the supplier that will be paid out the following month.

The right-hand side of the Balance Sheet contains two blocks which show where the finance from the left-hand side of the account has been used — what physical assets the company has obtained through the employment of the available finance.

Fixed assets are defined as the assets that the company owns and uses to carry on its business. Thus, the machine that John & Ben Ltd purchased is a fixed asset; so would be land and buildings, if the company owned any.

The second block is current assets. Current assets are items such as stock, debtors and cash that the company owns. They are distinct from fixed assets in that they will change quite rapidly as the company carries on its business. There will be a continual movement in the current assets of a company, and they should not be expected to stay static for long.

There is no statutory requirement as to how a company should show the financial information in its annual accounts. As long as the information is there, it does not matter how it is presented, though there are certain acceptable means of doing this which financial accountants have developed over the years. Today most companies show their Balance Sheet as illustrated in Fig. 2.2. This is the columnar or tabular form of presentation.

Fig. 2.2 *Balance sheet blocks*

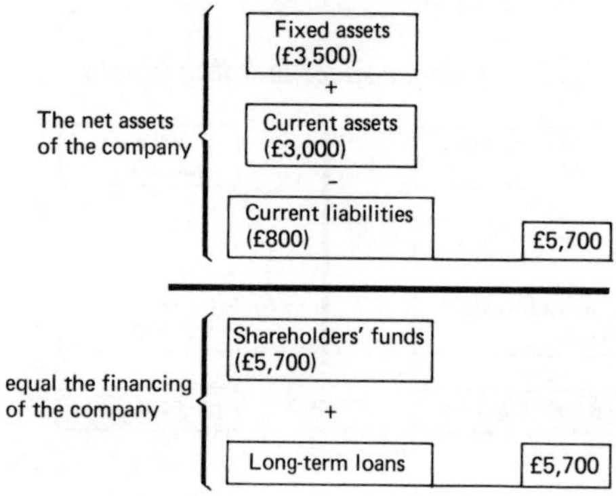

All that has been done in this changed presentation is to subtract from both sides of the Balance Sheet the current liabilities (£800). The current liabilities block is taken from the liabilities side of the Balance Sheet, and shown as a deduction from the assets side. In most cases, current liabilities are deducted from current assets to show the net current assets or the working capital of the company. The use of working capital will be covered in Chapter 3 but, briefly, it shows that a company has more current (short-term) assets than it has current (short-term) liabilities. The company can pay all its current liabilities out of its current assets without having either to sell fixed assets or raise loans.

The net assets of the company total £5,700. This equals the £5,700 of the shareholders' funds. Instead of the longer term liabilities of the company appearing on the opposite side of the page, these constitute the second change in the Balance Sheet presentation, by appearing underneath the net assets. In fact the Balance Sheet, still with exactly the same information in it, has been redrafted in a column. This is the format that is now commonly used by companies in their annual reporting.

2.5 THE ANNUAL ACCOUNTS OF A PUBLIC LIMITED COMPANY

To illustrate how a limited company presents a Profit and Loss Account and Balance Sheet to shareholders at the end of the financial year, the Annual Accounts of Currys Ltd are discussed. The principal activity of the Currys Group is retailing domestic electrical appliances, television, radio and audio equipment, and the company's year end is 24 January 1979. The accounts are termed 'consolidated' as the main company has a number of subsidiaries, and the financial figures for these subsidiaries are added together with those of the main company (consolidated) to provide a Profit and Loss Account and Balance Sheet (see Fig. 2.3).

The Profit and Loss Account for the year shows, in thousands of pounds, the turnover (revenue or sales income) generated during the year (£191.714m), with, as for all the other figures appearing in the accounts, comparative figures for the previous year. The company does not present a two-sided Profit and Loss Account of the type developed earlier in this chapter for John & Ben Ltd, but a single column of figures beginning with the year's turnover, and ending with the retained profit for the year (profit unappropriated for the year is £3.110m) which is added to the cumulative reserves in the Balance Sheet.

The first profit figure in the Profit and Loss Account is termed the 'Trading Profit' (£10.885m), and represents the profit the company has made from conducting its normal business. Some companies term this the 'Operating Profit'. Where a company makes a profit or a loss from some other activity then this will be shown separately in the Profit and Loss Account. An example of this is the surplus derived from the sale of properties (£0.352m). Currys is not in the business of buying and selling property, so the figure is shown separately from the Trading Profit. Some companies term such profits or losses as 'Extraordinary Items'.

At the foot of the Profit and Loss Account is the required statement of the earnings (profit) per share (34.7p). This is found by taking the profit attributable to the company for the year and dividing this by the number of ordinary shares in issue. SSAP 3 required that earnings per share (EPS) be shown in the Profit and Loss Account as an important indicator of the company's performance for the shareholder.

The Balance Sheet for Currys Ltd can be seen to contain the basic building blocks described above. The Fixed Assets (£20.014m) represent the physical investment in assets that are used to carry on the business. The Current Assets (£61.752m) are the assets of a short-term nature that will change from day to day as the company carries on its operations, and the Current Liabilities (£32.115m) show the short-term liabilities that the company is expected to pay out in the near future. As a guide, items that appear as Current Liabilities in a Balance Sheet can be taken as due for payment within the next twelve months. The amount of shareholders' funds (£50.125m) represents the long-term finance provided by shareholders of the company.

As part of the Annual Report and Accounts companies are expected to provide a statement of the accounting policies adopted in presenting the financial figures, and this is set out in the notes to the accounts (Fig. 2.4).

It can be seen from Note (c) in this statement that the company draws attention to a change in the method of treating deferred taxation. Accordingly those figures cannot be compared with the previous years, and the comparative figures for 1978 have been restated. The statement of accounting policies is provided to show how key figures in the accounts have been derived, and to provide those using the accounts with as much information as possible to assist their interpretation of the company's performance and state of affairs.

Fig. 2.3

Currys Limited

Consolidated Profit and Loss Account
Year ended 24th January 1979

	Note		1979 £'000		1978 £'000
Turnover	2		191,714		163,137
Trading profit	3		10,885		9,218
Interest receivable less payable	4		960		529
Surplus on sale of properties		603		571	
Less: Depreciation of buildings		251		—	
			352		571
Profit before taxation			12,197		10,318
Taxation:	7				
Charge on previous full deferral basis		6,532		5,309	
Less: Deferred taxation no longer provided		2,419		398	
			4,113		4,911
Profit available after taxation			8,084		5,407
Appropriated as follows:					
Inflation reserve	8	3,750		3,847	
Dividends	9	1,224		1,102	
			4,974		4,949
Profit unappropriated for year			3,110		458
Earnings per share	10		34.7p		22.9p

Fig. 2.3 continued

Balance Sheet
24th January 1979

	Note	1979 £'000	1978 £'000
Fixed assets	13	20,014	18,517
Advance corporation tax recoverable		474	560
Current assets:			
Stocks		29,541	24,773
Credit trading accounts	6	14,713	13,465
Trade and sundry debtors		1,648	1,494
Payments in advance		684	594
Short term deposits		14,350	13,975
Bank balances and cash		816	428
		61,752	54,729
Deduct:			
Current liabilities:			
Trade creditors and accrued expenses		27,296	24,632
Taxation		3,856	4,822
Preference dividend accrued		15	15
Proposed ordinary dividend	9	948	1,072
		32,115	30,541
Net current assets		29,637	24,188
Net assets		50,125	43,265
Financed by:			
Issued share capital	11	6,482	6,482
General reserves	12	25,970	22,860
Inflation reserve		17,673	13,923
Shareholders' funds		50,125	43,265

MICHAEL CURRY, *Joint Managing Director*
T. R. CURRY, *Joint Managing Director*
17th April, 1979.

The extent to which a company follows the various relevant SSAPs is a matter for discussion between the auditors and the directors, and can lead to fierce debate. For example H. W. Broad, the finance director of Trust Houses Forte Ltd, disagreed with the application of SSAP 12 to his

30

Fig. 2.4

Currys Limited

Notes to the Accounts

1 Accounting policies

(a) Group accounts
The Group accounts represent the consolidation of the accounts of the Holding Company and its subsidiaries, after the elimination of internal sales and profits, made up to 24th January, 1979 being the fourth Wednesday in January.

(b) Stocks
Valuation is based on current retail prices less a margin to reduce to cost having provided for obsolescence and deterioration.

(c) Credit trading
Profit is taken on credit trading as instalments are received and as a result profits in any one year are related to cash receipts.

(d) Depreciation of fixed assets
The Group's accounting policy in relation to the depreciation of buildings (not previously charged) has been changed to accord with the Statement of Standard Accounting Practice–Accounting for Depreciation (SSAP 12). Freehold properties and leasehold properties for a term exceeding 100 years unexpired are now depreciated at 2% per annum after elimination of the estimated site values. The remaining fixed assets are depreciated in equal annual instalments at rates calculated to spread the cost of the assets over their anticipated useful lives.

(e) Deferred taxation
The Group's accounting policy in relation to deferred taxation has been changed to accord with the Statement of Standard Accounting Practice – Accounting for Deferred Taxation (SSAP 15), and prior year figures have been restated accordingly. There is now no provision for deferred taxation which the Directors consider is unlikely to become payable in the foreseeable future; short term timing differences are given effect to in the accounts but, due to their relative immateriality, not separately disclosed.

(f) Inflation reserve
A transfer is made each year to inflation reserve to take cognizance of the effects of inflation on the Group's accounts and to mark the fact that this part of the Group profit cannot prudently be distributed by way of dividends.

(g) Property revaluation
The surplus arising on the revaluation referred to in the Directors' report has not been brought into these accounts.

company, and was reported[1] as stating: 'When accountants prepare general rules for everybody, they are not always properly applicable to every company . . . . Our job is to produce accounts which are sensible and meaningful to shareholders: our prime interest is not to be theoretical accountants'. Every set of accounts must have an Auditors' Report. In Currys' case there were two firms of auditors, so there is a joint report. This is shown in Fig. 2.5.

This Report draws attention to the fact that the Profit and Loss Account and Balance Sheet of the company have been prepared using the conventions of historic cost accounting, and that a separate set of accounts illustrating the impact of inflation on the company are provided elsewhere in the Annual Report (the current cost accounts).

The Auditors' Report also refers to 'source and application of funds' which is set out in a separate statement in the Annual Report. A more detailed discussion of this and SSAP 10 can be found in Chapter 5, where the Currys' 'Statement of Source and Application of Group Funds' is reproduced.

For public (quoted) companies the Stock Exchange has its own requirements for corporate financial reporting which, in some cases, extend the

---

Fig. 2.5

Report of the Joint Auditors
To the Members of Currys Limited

In our opinion the accounts of the Company and the Group which have been prepared in accordance with the historical cost convention, as set out on pages 9 to 17 inclusive, comply with the Companies Acts 1948 and 1967 and give, so far as concerns the members of Currys Limited, a true and fair view of the state of affairs at 24th January, 1979 and of the profit and source and application of funds for the year ended on that date.

We have also examined the supplementary statements on pages 18 and 19 prepared under the current cost accounting convention stated therein. In our opinion they fairly restate in summarised form the results for the year and financial position of the Group at 24th January, 1979 under that convention.

GRAHAM, SMART & ANNAN   HOGG, BULLIMORE & CO.
Chartered Accountants, Auditors   *Chartered Accountants, Auditors*
Hazlitt House, 28 Southampton Buildings, Chile House, 20 Ropemaker Street,
Chancery Lane, London WC2A 1AR   London EC2Y 9BA

17th April, 1979.

basic requirements of government legislation and accounting practice. The basic requirements of the Stock Exchange are set out in the 'Listing Agreement'. Quoted companies must keep the Stock Exchange Quotations Department up to date on their operations and activities through six-monthly reports (also sent to shareholders) and through other special notifications as necessary. Quoted companies are expected to adhere to the various accounting standards (SSAPs) and generally provide adequate financial information. There is also the *City Code on Takeovers and Mergers*[2] which provides detailed guidelines for the provision of information and the procedures to be followed during a merger or takeover. Where a company issues a prospectus to raise more capital the London Stock Exchange Quotations Department has laid down strict requirements as to the financial information which must be incorporated into such a prospectus.

2.6 THE USERS OF INFORMATION IN COMPANY ACCOUNTS

1975 saw the publication of both the 'Report of the Inflation Accounting Committee' (Sandilands)[3] and *The Corporate Report* by the Accounting Standards Steering Committee (ASSC).[4] Whilst each had different objectives, they both considered such questions as: Who uses the Annual Reports of companies? and What information do they need? Interested user groups include the following:

(i) *Shareholders.* They will receive a copy of the Annual Report which is a statement of the directors' stewardship of their investment in the company. Many companies now make use of the Annual Report to illustrate their products, and in many cases colour photographs abound. The shareholder, if he reads the report, will probably be concerned with the growth in revenue and profit of the company, as well as the dividend the directors are proposing to pay. However, the majority of small shareholders do not rely on the Annual Report for an assessment of the company, but rather on analyses and comments in the financial press.

(ii) *Potential shareholders.* They will be looking at the same information as existing shareholders, and again are most likely to rely on professional advice or newspaper comment for their assessment of the viability of company's shares as an investment. Public companies' annual reports are usually widely available, in specialist libraries, or from the companies themselves.

(iii) *Investment analysts.* These advise investors and, as such, are mainly concerned with future prospects. It is not much help from the investment point of view to know what profit the company made last year, since it is too late to do anything about it. Past performance is only useful as evidence for future capability. Thus, investment analysts will give only brief time to the historic accounts of the company, and devote most of their effort to an assessment of its potential for growth and profit. This will entail an analysis of the economy and the industry in which the company operates, as well as a detailed assessment of the management of the company. The Annual Report is just the starting-off point for analysis; it is the hors d'oeuvre, not the main course.

(iv) *Bankers.* The banker who provides overdraft facilities to a company will wish to be kept informed as to its operations, and will receive a copy of the Annual Report. The main concern will be whether the money advanced will be repaid as expected. The bank manager is probably the last professional to place reliance on the Annual Report for information for decision-making on a company. But this is changing as bankers become more educated as to what businessmen actually do, and what information is really necessary to monitor company performance.

(v) *Customers.* A few of the company's customers will be interested in the Annual Report. This is sensible where they are considering placing a large order, and require to know how financially sound the company is. They will need reassurance that it will be in business next year to service the product that has been purchased. This is especially the case where long-term supply contracts are concerned.

(vi) *Employees.* Not many employees spend time studying their company's Annual Report. But many companies are trying to use their report as a means of communicating with their employees. The whole range of the company's products can be set out, as well as information that employees would not normally see in their work with a single section of the company. The chairman can direct his comments to employees to explain the company's philosophy, or the likely impact of some social change or new piece of legislation. An example of a recent Employment Report is shown in Section 2.7.

(vii) *Trade Unions.* Trade Unions have research departments which can analyse a set of accounts as competently as the management side. They will be interested in the employment implications of growth, diversification and new technology, and the way in which profit is used. The 1975 Employment Protection Act and the Advisory Conciliation and Arbitration Service (ACAS) *Code of Practice* in 1977[5] dealing with the disclosure of information to trade unions for collective bargaining purposes considerably increased the amount of information that may be made available to unions in addition to the normal published company reports. Of course one must expect a union, for bargaining purposes, to interpret the accounts in the light most favourable to their own case. And often they will be better informed via their members on the detailed operating realities than many senior managers.

(viii) *Creditors.* These will be rating the company on its creditworthiness and concerned as to whether they will receive payment. Their concern will be with the solvency or liquidity of the company, as well as future sales potential.

(ix) *Management.* The Annual Report can be used as an effective communication tool by directors, and the managers in the company will probably give some attention to what is said there. They will also be able to see how their bit of the company's operations fits into the overall picture.

The directors will certainly study the Annual Report, and two of them sign it. But they will be mainly concerned with its preparation, and trying to assess how it will be received by those people who will read, analyse and comment on it. They will not be trying to run the company on the basis of the Annual Report. Any board of directors that has to wait until the annual accounts are prepared to discover if they made a profit or a loss during the year can hardly be said to be in control.

(x) *The General Public.* With the current increased emphasis on the social responsibilities of business, one must expect the general public (often via the media) to demand information on its activities in the society or locality affected by its operations — particularly where these involve environmental changes.

(xi) *Government and Official Bodies.* Governments require access to information on companies operating within a country both for economic and social planning purposes, and also for statistical monitoring. Often companies are requested to complete special returns on particular aspects of their operations for government bodies. Not least, of course, the government needs information for taxation collection purposes. Since 1975 the requirement to produce returns on Value Added Tax, and keep the appropriate records, has generated an additional book-keeping burden, particularly for small companies. But in general, with the proliferation of interested Government and other various official departments, companies receive unco-ordinated requests for information from many sources.

(xii) *Competitors.* Other companies will be looking at the published information of their competitors to try to gain insights on future plans and policies and for comparative performance analysis. The Confederation of British Industry (CBI) in evidence to The Sandilands Committee described five main reasons for other companies needing such information ('Report of the Inflation Accounting Committee' 1975, paragraph 180):

(i) for financial analysis and comparison;
(ii) to check the creditworthiness of customers or suppliers;
(iii) to monitor competition;
(iv) for portfolio investment, for example, by pension funds; and
(v) for research into intended mergers or acquisitions.

All these user groups are looking to the company to produce information relevant to their needs, and it is unlikely that a single set of financial statements could satisfy all their differing requirements. Presumably a firm would rather produce no (or misleading) information for its competitors' requirements. However, for the future it can be expected that companies will be required to provide more information rather than less. In fulfilling this requirement companies will be expected to ensure that all their reports meet certain basic criteria. They should be, according to the *Corporate Report* (para 3.3):

Relevant	Complete
Understandable	Objective
Reliable	Timely
	Comparable.

2.7 THE FUTURE OF CORPORATE REPORTING

Companies, in the sense of associations of individuals for the purpose of trade or manufacture, have been operating for a long time, in many societies. For production or manufacture, they would often be based on a family unit, or grouped round a master craftsman. Such groups and partnerships occurred in classical Greece and Rome. Brutus for instance, the honourable man, was part of a financial syndicate which, among other business, subcontracted to collect taxes from the people of Cyprus, charging interest at extortionate rates. In Stone-Age Britain, evidence from Grimes Graves suggests that this flint mine was a large joint operation sending flints many miles afield. Subsequent trade and commerce would have required similar joint endeavours. The term 'Company' was used formally in the founding of the East India Company in 1600, and the Hudson's Bay Company in 1670, but these unlimited liability companies bear little resemblance to the modern limited liability company. Gradually

the formal approach to financial reporting by companies was introduced —
for example the Joint Stock Companies Act of 1844 and 1855 — and
developed through the application of professional standards by the accounting profession (as discussed in Chapter 1) and more recent legislation
(Companies Acts of 1948, 1967 and 1976). Behind all these developments
was the pressure to satisfy the needs and protect the interests of those who
use the information contained in the financial reports of companies. In
1975 the *Corporate Report* stated:

> The fundamental objective of corporate reports is to communicate
> economic measurements of and information about, the resources and
> performance of the reporting entity useful to those having reasonable
> rights to such information.

The *Corporate Report* suggested several additional statements that companies might produce with their traditional accounts in the Annual Report.

(a) Value Added Statement

A value added statement is shown in Appendix 2 from the 1979 Annual
Report of Pilkington Brothers Ltd, a group whose business is the manufacture and marketing of glass and glass products. Value Added is an increas-
ingly popular method of presenting financial information in a relatively
simple and straightforward manner, and proves useful in avoiding a
misunderstanding of 'profit' as shown in traditional reports. The value
added statement for Pilkington Brothers first shows the value added in
millions of pounds, from trading activities (£289.7) and other sources
(£46) to give a total of £335.7. The way this has been distributed, or used
by the group, is then shown under the main headings of Payroll (employee
costs) of £194.9, Taxation (£42.7) and the amount ploughed back into the
business for reinvestment (£81.5). This form of presentation is a useful
addition in that it shows where the company generates money and how
this is used. A more detailed discussion of value added statements is to be
found in Appendix 2. At the foot of the Pilkington statement are a series
of 'key ratios' showing average figures per employee. These provide clues
to salary and wage inflation, and to changes in productivity over time.

(b) Employment Report

The *Corporate Report* also recommended the provision of an 'Employment
Report' to provide information on the working relationship the company
has with its employees. As an example, the 1979 Employment Report is
shown for Marks & Spencer Ltd, a company which traditionally has
prided itself on its good human relations (Fig. 2.6).

Fig. 2.6

EMPLOYMENT REPORT FOR THE COMPANY (MARKS AND SPENCER LTD) FOR THE YEAR ENDED 31st MARCH, 1979

The average number of employees was 43,968 including 26,308 part-timers. This is the equivalent of 29,519 full-time employees.

Absence for sickness and domestic reasons averaged 4.5% of total numbers (*last year 4.2%*).

Over 40% of our staff have been with us for over five years.

During the coming year the number of staff who will have achieved 25 years service with the Company will total over 5,000 whilst more than 500 will have reached 40 years service. The Board recognise these long service achievements with presentations at our Head Office.

The Company's Employment Policy—Equal Opportunities

The sole criterion for selection or promotion in the Company is suitability for the job. The highest positions are open to all—we do not discriminate on the grounds of colour, race, religion or sex.

We now employ both men and women in positions which were once held by only one sex. We have over 100 women training for Store Management. We employ women as merchandisers and technologists in Head Office and men as Sales Assistants and Supervisors in our Stores.

Minimum Income Level

The minimum cost of employing an 18 year old sales assistant with one year's satisfactory service is now over £3,700 per annum of which over £2,650 is salary and bonus. Many earn more. The £3,700 includes statutory payments such as National Insurance contributions and company benefits such as non-contributory pension scheme, subsidised catering and health services.

Profit Sharing

98% of employees participating in last year's Profit Sharing Scheme have retained their shares.

This year the Company, subject to Shareholder approval, will take advantage of the tax concessions under the 1978 Finance Act by offering employees a choice of either participating in a new 'delayed' share scheme or of remaining in the original 'immediate' share scheme. By law tax

Fig. 2.6 *continued*

concessions under the proposed 'delayed' scheme are conditional upon the employee agreeing to hold the shares for a minimum period of five years.

Social Involvement

The Company is conscious of its social involvement in the community it serves.

Each year the Company encourages its employees to support a charity through various fund raising events. Over the last nine years over £¼ million has been raised through these 'Miss Sparks' charity events. This is in addition to various Charities 'adopted' and supported by individual Stores.

Staff Welfare

A priority of the Staff Management team of over 700 people in our Stores and Head Office is to counsel and assist our staff with their problems.

In addition, a Welfare Committee, originally formed in 1933, meets each week to offer help and advice to members of our staff with major health or welfare problems. Over 240 cases were considered during the year.

Pensions

We had 4,685 pensioners at the end of March 1979. Retirements during the year totalled 564.

To finance employees' non-contributory pensions the Company made payments into the Pension Scheme totalling over £18 million for the year.

We continue to run 'in Company' seminars to help equip staff going into retirement to adjust to their new life style.

(c) Statement of money exchanges with Government
The *Corporate Report* recommended that more precise details of the relationship with Central and Local Government should be disclosed. The 1979 Marks & Spencer Ltd statement is one example (Fig. 2.7).

The *Corporate Report* (para. 6.42) also recommended the presentation of a statement of transactions in foreign currency, a statement of future prospects, as forecast by company management, and a statement of Corporate Objectives which should include statements of the philosophy or policy and strategic targets of the company in the following areas:

Sales	Employment
Added Value	Consumer Issues
Profitability	Environmental Matters
Investment and Finance	Other relevant social issues.
Dividends	

Fig. 2.7

FINANCIAL RELATIONSHIP WITH U.K. CENTRAL AND LOCAL GOVERNMENT

	1979 £'000	1978 £'000
Corporation tax on the year's profits amounted to.	75,150	53,900
In addition to the above the following central and local government charges have also been borne by the Company:—		
Rates	11,728	11,163
Import duty	2,273	2,487
Contribution for national insurance	9,134	8,589
Total cost to the Company of U.K. central and local government charges.	98,285	76,139
The Company is also obliged to collect the following taxes for which they are accountable to the U.K. government:—		
Value added tax on sales.	71,113	58,840
Income tax deducted from employees' salaries	18,206	16,884
Income tax deducted from interest on debenture stocks.	1,048	1,080
Employee contributions for national insurance	3,651	3,701
Making a total for the year for which the Company is accountable to U.K. central and local government of	192,303	156,644

The topic of Social Accounting, which is 'the reporting of those costs and benefits, which may or may not be quantifiable in money terms, arising from economic activities and substantially borne or received by the community at large, or particular groups not holding a direct relationship with the reporting entity' (para 6.46), was seen as an area of growing concern to the accounting profession. The problem here is how far reasonably accurate identification and measurement of the actual social costs and benefits deriving from an organisation's operations or policies can be achieved in this area.

Sir Ronald Leach in his foreword to the *Corporate Report*, described it as

> intended to be the starting point of a major review of the users, purposes and methods of modern financial reporting. It is a first step, not the last word.

It has certainly stimulated debate[6] on the whole subject of financial reporting, and may be expected to provide the basis from which future developments in corporate reporting derive.

3 The Analysis of Annual Accounts

In our first two chapters the basic principles, concepts, terminology, and conventions of financial accounting have been introduced. But before practical analysis of a set of Accounts can be undertaken it is necessary to appreciate the full scope of the information in a company's Annual Report.

3.1 THE ANNUAL REPORT AND THE BALANCE SHEET

Every company is required each year to provide a Profit and Loss Account (or an Income and Expenditure Account), together with a Balance Sheet. These must be presented to shareholders, and to others with a long-term interest in the company (such as debenture holders) at least twenty-one days prior to the Annual General Meeting of the company.

The 1948 Companies Act defined the information to be contained in the Annual Report, and this has been updated by the 1967 and 1976 Companies Acts. The general guide provided by the 8th Schedule of the 1948 Act together with Sections 147–58 gives the basis for all companies' reports. There is no particular layout or design of accounts prescribed by the Act. All that is statutorily defined is the information that must be contained in each report.

The Annual Report must contain not only the Profit and Loss Account and Balance Sheet of the company, but also the Directors' Report. The contents of the Directors' Report are set out in Sections 16–20 of the 1967 Companies Act. In broad terms these are:

(i) A report as to the 'state of the company's affairs'. This is taken to mean a statement of the profit generated for the year.

(ii) What dividends the directors are proposing for the year, and the amounts to be retained in the company by creating or adding to reserves in the Balance Sheet.

   (iii) A statement of the directors' shareholding in the company, including shares held by wives and children, and those held as trustee.

   (iv) A statement of changes in membership of the Board.

   (v) A statement of the average number of employees of the company and their total remuneration.

   (vi) Where the current value of land held by the company is substantially different from that shown in the Balance Sheet, the directors must disclose this fact.

   (vii) A statement of charitable and political contributions made during the year – unless they total less than £50.

   (viii) The amount of revenue generated from exporting.

The Annual Report will also normally contain a Chairman's Statement to the shareholders in which he outlines the past year's operations and makes any comments he feels necessary. Often this covers a review of the year and brief discussion of the major areas of the company's business. The Annual Accounts of the company will have an Auditors' Report, which must conform to Section 149 of the 1948 Act, requiring that every Balance Sheet presented 'shall give a true and fair view of the state of affairs of the company as at the end of its financial year' and, as in the Currys' Auditors' Report, will also cover the Profit and Loss Account, and a Sources and Application of Funds Statement (see Chapter 2, Section 2.5).

Thus a typical Annual Report can be expected to contain the following information:

   (i) Names of directors of the company;

   (ii) Names of the company's bankers, auditors, solicitors and other relevant professionals;

   (iii) The address of the company's registered office;

   (iv) Notice of the calling of the Annual General Meeting to consider the Accounts;

   (v) Directors' Report;

   (vi) Chairman's Statement;

   (vii) Profit and Loss Account for the year;

   (viii) Balance Sheet for the end of the year signed by two directors;

   (ix) Statement of Accounting Policies;

   (x) Auditors' Report;

   (xi) Notes on the Accounts where required, to comply with the Companies Acts;

   (xii) Source and Application of Funds Statement;

(xiii) Current Cost Statement;
(xiv) Details of subsidiary and associated companies.

Often companies provide further information in the Annual Report, such as a five-year record of the business, and other statements. Examples of some additional statements adopted by companies were illustrated in Chapter 2.

Schedule Eight of the 1948 Companies Act specifies that in a Balance Sheet, 'The authorised share capital, issued share capital, liabilities, and assets shall be summarised, with such particulars as are necessary to disclose the general nature of the assets and liabilities'.

The 1979 Balance Sheet of Currys (Chapter 2, Section 2.5) can be seen to contain the major building blocks used in the development of John & Ben Ltd's accounts in Chapter 2.

$$\text{Fixed Assets} + (\text{Current Assets} - \text{Current Liabilities}) = \text{Net Assets}$$

and

$$\text{Share Capital} + \text{Reserves} = \text{Capital Employed.}$$

In Curry's balance sheet advance corporation tax (£0.474m) must be included in the Net Asset figure and, as the company has no external long-term borrowing the net assets are financed completely by Shareholders' Funds (share capital + reserves). The two sections of the Balance Sheet show where the company obtained its finance (capital employed) and how it has used it (net assets). Or, more simply, where the money has come from, and where it has gone.

Each of the major blocks in the Balance Sheet will now be considered in detail. When the reader has understood these first three chapters, he should be able to interpret and understand any company's Balance Sheet.

3.2 FIXED ASSETS AND DEPRECIATION

The first heading on the Currys' Balance Sheet is 'Fixed Assets'. For Currys this represents the properties, fixtures and fittings, and vehicles used by the company. Fixed assets are a semi-permanent investment in physical items – the physical assets that the company will use to carry on its business. These assets will be held for a number of years, added to and deducted from, as the company carries on its operations. A fixed asset will not contain items that the company trades in. For example, with a garage the stock of cars held for sales to customers will not be treated as a fixed asset — they will appear in the inventory — but the breakdown vehicle that the garage uses to collect cars will appear as a fixed asset, because it is used in the business and will be held for a number of years. The fixed assets enable the business to be conducted; they are not bought and sold for operating profit.

One of the basic accounting concepts in Chapter 1 was historic cost valuation. This applies in dealing with the fixed assets. The original cost of the asset is entered into the Balance Sheet, and has depreciation set against it. The only time cost is not used is when the company has revalued its assets, and then the revaluation figure is used in the Balance Sheet.

In arriving at the £20.014m valuation of Fixed Assets for Currys, depreciation of £8.684m has been deducted from the original cost (or most recent valuation). This is found from reading Note 13 relating to the Accounts. There are several ways of handling depreciation. The basic principle is that wear and tear on the fixed assets must be brought into the company's accounts when determining profit. If during the year's operations some of the life of the physical assets has been used up, this should be taken as a 'cost' against the year's revenues. The charging each year in the Profit and Loss Account of an amount to cover depreciation of the assets ensures no reduction in the capital employed. If depreciation were not charged in the accounts, a false profitability would result.

One distinguished academic had an unpleasant experience which underlines the problems of understanding depreciation. As a junior articled clerk he was given the audit of a working mens' club. He balanced the accounts and was sent along to the meeting to present them to the members of the club. He asked if there were any questions on the accounts, and was asked, 'Where's the depreciation gone?' From the layman, a sensible question, but for the trainee accountant very difficult to answer convincingly. In the case of Currys there has been deducted from the Profit and Loss Account £8.684m over the life of the properties and plant, and in the Balance Sheet £8.684m has been deducted from the valuation of Fixed Assets. So where has the depreciation gone? The answer is that we do not know. It has been used in the business along with all the other funds generated from operations and retained in the company. There is no separate account with cash from depreciation in it. The depreciation, as part of the total cashflow generated by the company, has been retained in the business, and it is impossible to separate depreciation pounds from pounds of retained profit. What is certain is that if depreciation is not charged, there will be no facility for replacing worn-out assets and failure to charge depreciation will reduce the shareholders' equity proportionately.

However, it is an accounting convention, though a realistic one, that shows depreciation as a deduction from Fixed Assets in the Balance Sheet.

It would be possible to redraft Currys' Balance Sheet thus:

	£'000s
Fixed assets at cost or valuation	28,698
Advance corporation tax	474
Net current assets	29,637
Net assets	58,809
Shareholders' funds	50,125
Accumulated depreciation	8,684
Capital employed	58,809

In this redrafted Balance Sheet the properties, fixtures and fittings, computer and motor vehicles are shown on the assets side, and the accumulated depreciation shown on the liabilities side. The accumulated depreciation shows a setting aside of some of the profit to allow for wear and tear on the assets, and it is retained in the business in just the same way as the retained profit. Of the many ways of calculating depreciation, the three most common are:

(i) *Straight-line method.* This is the simplest to operate. The depreciation charge is calculated by taking the historic cost of the asset, and dividing it by the anticipated life of the asset.

(ii) *Reducing-balance method.* Under this method a constant percentage of the asset balance is deducted.

(iii) *Sum-of-the digits method.* This method takes the anticipated life of the asset as the basis, and weights its early years most heavily. Thus if the anticipated life is 10 years, all the digits 1, 2, 3, 4, 5, 6, 7, 8, 9, 10 are added together to give 55. In the first year 10/55ths are charged for the depreciation, in the second year 9/55ths, and so on until the final year has 1/55th charged for depreciation.

The method most difficult to calculate is the reducing-balance method, where the percentage to apply each year to the balance of the asset value must be found. There is a general formula which assists in this:

$$\text{Depreciation rate} = 1 - \sqrt[n]{\frac{\text{Scrap value}}{\text{Original cost}}}$$

where n = number of years of anticipated life.

However, the problem with this approach is the estimation of scrap value. Most companies which use this method assess a reasonable rate of depreciation and apply that to the assets. In the table below we assume a

46

20 per cent rate, twice the particular straight-line method rate. The three methods are compared in the table in the case of a machine costing £1,000, with an anticipated life of ten years.

DEPRECIATION CHARGE

Year	Straight-line	Sum-of-digits	Reducing balance
1	100	182	200
2	100	164	160
3	100	145	128
4	100	127	102
5	100	109	82
6	100	91	66
7	100	73	52
8	100	55	42
9	100	36	34
10	100	18	27
	£1,000	£1,000	£893

Under the reducing-balance method there is still £107 of the asset to be written off after ten years. Under this method it is impossible to depreciate an asset completely for there will always be some balance of the reducing total left (and the formula assumes a scrap value greater than zero).

The charging of depreciation in the Profit and Loss Account will have an impact on the annual profit. If the table had related to three different firms each of which was making a steady £1,000 profit each year, then each would be showing a different 'profit'. Depreciation is to some extent an arbitrary assessment by management, but its results are seen directly in the profit retained. It is important to remember this when studying company reports. The depreciation figure should be considered to see if it is reasonable, and if the method is consistent over time and between companies. The difficulties of incorporating the impact of inflation on the depreciation charge are considered in Chapter 4.

Currys' Balance Sheet shows a figure of £20.014m for the book value of properties and plant. What does this figure convey? Is it, for instance:

(i) the market value of the assets if sold?
(ii) the replacement cost of the assets?
(iii) how much the company would be willing to sell the assets for?

The £20.014m is none of those values. It merely shows that the assets cost (or have been revalued at) a certain amount, and since then have been depreciated by a certain amount, to provide the book value as stated. This is the figure appearing as a balance in the books of the company on 24 January 1979. It is more of an accountants' book-keeping figure than anything else; it is used to ensure that the Balance Sheet balances.

In looking at a Balance Sheet, the date upon which the assets were purchased, or revalued, should be taken into account. But until inflation accounting is fully operational this will be a difficult task as few Annual Reports provide sufficient data to enable this to be done adequately.

3.3 CURRENT ASSETS

(a) Stock
The 1967 Companies Act states (Schedule 2):

> If the amount carried forward for stock in trade, or work in progress, is material for the appreciation by its members of the company's state of affairs, or of its profit or loss for the financial year, the manner in which that amount has been computed . . . shall be stated by way of note, or in a statement or report annexed, if not otherwise shown.

For most companies the value of stock is materially important, so they must define how they have arrived at the value of stock shown in the year-end Balance Sheet, usually in the statement of accounting policies in the Annual Report. In the case of Currys the method is described as taking the current retail price of goods less 'a margin to reduce to cost having provided for obsolescence and deterioration'. A more common valuation method for stock in the UK is to take the value as cost or net realisable value, whichever is the lower. Valuation of stock is a very important factor in company reporting, yet most professional accountants would probably agree that stock is the most difficult figure on a Balance Sheet to verify. It includes verification both of the physical identities and quantities, and of their values. In the case of a retail organisation it seems a comparatively easy task. At the year end (assuming reasonable record-keeping) the stock of goods in each store can be calculated quite accurately, and this can be added to the value of goods in the pipeline to provide the total stock on hand at the auditing date. However, whilst the mechanics are quite easy, the physical size of the task can be gauged from the fact that the group has some 475 retail outlets as well as large warehousing and service facilities.

In all companies the stock figure is a valuation, and the end figure for stock in the Balance Sheet depends upon the valuation basis. Stock is important not only for a proper assessment of capital employed in the business, but also in the calculation of profit in the Profit and Loss Account.

Profit is arrived at by deducting costs plus expenses, from the revenue for the year. A substantial part of the costs for most companies are the materials purchased and used to produce the products that are sold. Take a simple example:

Revenue		£2,000
Opening stock	1,000	
add Purchases	1,000	
	2,000	
less Closing stock	1,000	
Cost of Goods Sold		1,000
Gross Profit		£1,000

If the value of the closing stock is increased by £500 (to £1,500), then the profit for the year becomes £1,500, an equal increase of £500. If the closing stock were valued at £500, then the profit would be £500. This extreme example illustrates the impact of stock valuation on profitability, and shows why the valuation of stock can be so important a factor in company performance and financial status.

The auditor must watch for inconsistencies in stock valuation, but it is not realistic to expect a complete verification of all stocks. He must rely on the company's figures and records. Auditors use statistical sampling methods in verifying stock, and will normally check at least a proportion of the total stock at the year end. But the auditor is rarely fully conversant with the technology of the business he is dealing with. He cannot be expected to differentiate between special chemicals, steels, parts, sub-assemblies etc., and therefore must depend on the personnel of the company during stocktaking exercises.

The stock figure in the Balance Sheet will include:

  (i) raw materials as yet unused;
 (ii) work-in-progress (part-finished products);
(iii) finished products ready for sale.

The majority of companies provide only a single figure for this composite group, which is not always sufficient if one is an outsider trying to analyse in detail.

The type of problem which can arise in stock valuation has been highlighted in the case of D. F. Bevan (Holdings) Ltd's accounts, where an employee of the company altered the directors' stock figures, so that the final valuations were based partly on fictitious stock levels. The employee was not acting for personal gain, but the accounts prepared on the basis of these stock figures overstated the real profitability of the company.

(b) Methods of stock valuation

A company will usually have records of what it has purchased during the year, and (depending on its stock control records) how much has been used in goods sold, but the valuation of closing stock will depend on the cost at which purchased materials have been transferred to production.

If the price of the company's raw material does not alter during the year, then there is no problem. But the price of most goods fluctuates during the year, and therefore most companies have to choose a method of valuing their stock. There are three main methods of stock valuation, as illustrated below. There are also other methods such as standard cost and direct cost which will be considered in Chapters 9 and 10.

(i) *First in first out (FIFO) method.* This method assumes that the items longest in stock are used first, hence the name. As stock is used, it is charged to production at the earliest price.

Cost of materials purchased:

1,000 lb of metal @ £5 per lb =		5,000
1,000 lb of metal @ £6 per lb =		6,000
2,000 lb at total cost of		£11,000

less Amount used in production

1,000 lb @ £5 per lb =	5,000	
500 lb @ £6 per lb =	3,000	
1,500		8,000
Closing Stock: 500 lb @ £6 per lb =		£3,000

Under this method of stock valuation the closing stock of material is close to the replacement cost if prices are rising.

(ii) *Last in first out (LIFO) method.* This method of stock valuation is the reverse of FIFO. Using the same details as above, the stock valuation becomes:

Cost of materials purchased		£11,000
less Amount used in production		
1,000 lb @ £6 per lb =	6,000	
500 lb @ £5 per lb =	2,500	8,500
Closing Stock: 500 lb @ £5 per lb =		£2,500

Using LIFO under conditions of rising prices will undervalue the stock on hand, but value the cost of goods sold at a higher amount than under FIFO.

(iii) *Average cost method*. This method uses the average of the price of materials purchased. Using the same figures as previously, the stock valuation becomes:

Cost of materials purchased   £11,000

$$\text{Average cost} = \frac{£11,000}{2,000 \text{ lb}} = £5.5 \text{ per lb}$$

Closing Stock: 500 lb @ £5.5 per lb = £2,750

(c) Comparison of the Three Methods

		FIFO	*LIFO*	*Average*
Sales income for period		£10,000	10,000	10,000
Cost of goods sold:				
Opening stock	—		—	—
Purchases	£11,000		11,000	11,000
	11,000		11,000	11,000
Closing stock	(3,000)		(2,500)	(2,750)
Cost of goods sold		8,000	8,500	8,250
Gross profit for period		£2,000	1,500	1,750

Different methods of stock valuation produce different profit figures. But if the company is consistent in its stock valuation method, as required by one of the basic conventions of accountancy, the long-term difference will be zero, in that the above closing stock values eventually find their way through to profits. Note that this disregards considerations of inflation.

	FIFO	LIFO	Average
Sales for next period	£5,000	5,000	5,000
Cost of goods sold:			
Opening stock 3,000	2,500	2,750	
Purchases —			
3,000	2,500	2,750	
Closing stock —	—	—	
Cost of goods sold	3,000	2,500	2,750
Gross profit for period	£2,000	2,500	2,750
Gross profit for first period	2,000	1,500	1,750
Gross profit for second period	2,000	2,500	2,250
	£4,000	£4,000	£4,000

(d) Debtors and Prepayments

The next items in Currys Balance Sheet are concerned with customers and other parties who have incurred some financial obligation to the company.

Debtors arise where a company has allowed customers credit facilities. The customer is allowed a certain time before he has to pay for the goods he has received. A typical situation is where a company allows 30 days before it expects customers to pay.

If a company feels that some of its debtors will either not pay at all, or only in part, then allowance must be made for this in the calculation of year-end debtors. A provision is made for bad or doubtful debts, and deducted from the total debtor figure. The amount appearing in the Balance Sheet as debtors represents debts that the company expects to receive in the near future. If there is any unusual movement in bad debts, such as a major customer going into liquidation, then the Annual Report will contain information on this, or otherwise explain why the provision for doubtful debts has been substantially increased.

In the case of a mainly retail operation with customers paying cash there will be relatively few debtors. Where customer credit facilities are offered as part of the company's market strategy, the amount owed by such customers at the year end is shown in the Balance Sheet. With Currys this was a larger figure (£14.713m) than ordinary trade and sundry debtors (£1.648m).

Prepayments, or payments in advance (£0.684m) arise when a company pays for a service for some time ahead. For example, rent, rates and insurance are often paid for a year in advance. The amount paid during this year relates to benefits to be received in the following year. Thus, if the Balance Sheet date of a company falls just after the insurance premiums have been paid for the next twelve months, this amount cannot be shown as an expense against the current year's revenue, but must be set aside as a current asset, and termed a prepayment.

(e) Bank Balances and Cash

Currys show £0.816m either as cash or in the bank at the end of the year. This represents the amount of truly liquid resources the company had available at the end of the year. This may not of course be a figure typical of the rest of the year. The Balance Sheet is made up at a certain point in time, and the cash position shown merely represents the liquid resources on hand at that time. Retail stores usually have surplus liquid resources at certain periods. For instance, if a company will need to use cash in the future (for example to pay the tax bill, or invest in more assets), but has no immediate need for all its cash in hand, it can put its cash to some constructive and profitable use until it is needed, by investing in short-term instruments. Thus Currys have £14.35m of Short-term Deposits shown in their Balance Sheet. They have invested their surplus liquid resources for a short period to earn interest. Where an investment or deposit is shown in Current Assets it indicates a short-term use of available liquid funds. If an investment or deposit is shown between the Fixed Assets and the Current Asset in the Balance Sheet it indicates a longer term policy investment.

3.4 CURRENT LIABILITIES

Currys show £27.296m for *creditors and accrued expenses* at the end of the year. Under Creditors appear the goods and services provided during the year which have yet to be paid for. The company owes this amount. Creditors are the reverse of debtors, who owe the company money for goods or services they have received during the year.

Often the term 'Accrued Charges' or 'Accrued Expenses' appears in the Current Liabilities section. These are the opposite of prepayments. For example, rent may be due at the year end but has not yet been paid, as may also apply to electricity and telephone charges. These expenses must be shown in the Profit and Loss Account even though they have not yet entered the company's books, and also appear in the Balance Sheet as current liabilities. If a company has a *bank overdraft* at the Balance Sheet date, this will appear as part of Current Liabilities because it is a short-term source of finance. The overdraft is, at least in theory (see Chapter 6), repayable to the bank on demand, and so must be shown in this section of the Balance Sheet. The overdraft position shown in the Balance Sheet may not be representative of the rest of the year. It is merely the balance existing at the end of the year when the Balance Sheet is drawn up.

Where loans or other borrowings are shown within the Current Liabilities section of the Balance Sheet, this indicates short-term borrowings which may be expected to be repaid within the coming year.

Where *taxation* appears as a current liability it indicates that this amount will be paid to the Inland Revenue within the next twelve months. For most companies this will be tax on the previous year's profits, as there is approximately a year's lag between incurring the liability and having to pay it.

3.5 DIVIDENDS AND SHAREHOLDERS' FUNDS

Currys show *dividends* of £0.015m due to preference shareholders and £0.948m, due to ordinary shareholders at the year end. Ordinary and Preference shares are discussed in Chapter 6. The £0.948m represents the final dividend to the ordinary shareholders which the directors are to propose at the Annual General Meeting. From the Profit and Loss Account, £1.224m is shown for dividends, so an interim dividend has also been paid. The £0.948m is the amount the company proposes to pay to shareholders at the year end. This will be paid immediately after the Annual General Meeting if the directors' recommendations for dividends are accepted.

The final section in Currys' Balance Sheet shows the *shareholders' funds* invested in the company. This is made up of the share capital provided by the shareholders (Note 11 on the Accounts provides information as to both the authorised and issued share capital of the company). There are one million preference shares of £1 each, and £6.3m of 25p ordinary shares authorised: 660,386 preference shares have been issued, and £5,821,875 of 25p ordinary shares giving the total Issued Share Capital of £6.482m. The General Reserves (£25.97m) have come from the Profit and Loss Accounts of the Company, mainly in the form of retained profits ploughed back into the company over its life. Information on Currys' Inflation Reserve can be found by reading the statement of Accounting Policies (Chapter 2, Section 2.5).

3.6 OTHER BALANCE SHEET ITEMS

(a) Debentures and other long-term debt
The Currys' Balance Sheet shows no long-term loans, but where a company uses this type of capital it appears as one of the basic Balance Sheet building blocks as illustrated in Fig 2.1. The different kinds of debenture, and the notion of gearing or leverage (the relationship between fixed

54

interest capital and equity capital) are discussed in Chapter 6. For Balance Sheet analysis it should be noted that loans for over a year are classified as long-term; that bank overdrafts, being repayable on demand, count as short-term liabilities; and that the annual interest charges on debt are part of the operating expenses deductible from turnover in the Profit and Loss Account.

(b) Group and consolidated accounts

Most public companies are groups, that is, two or more companies trading together under a main company's ownership or control. The 1948 Companies Act requires that shareholders be provided with full information on a group's activities, so in the Annual Report of a group will appear:

   (i) Group Profit and Loss Account (Consolidated);
  (ii) Group Balance Sheet (Consolidated);
 (iii) Main company Balance Sheet.

With a group there will be two Balance Sheets, the main one listing the assets and liabilities of all companies within the group, and the other showing the financial standing of the parent or main company. The Group Consolidated Profit and Loss Account shows the sum of the trading activities of all companies concerned.

Consolidated means that all the figures have been brought together. All sales to outside customers by the various companies are added together, as are their costs, to provide the overall Profit and Loss Account. The Balance Sheet is the total of the assets and liabilities of all companies in the group. Most of the useful information for analysis will appear in the group consolidated accounts, not in the main company Balance Sheet.

The preparation of consolidated accounts is an involved task. The following simple example illustrates the way in which such accounts are produced.

Marx Ltd and Spengler Ltd are two independent companies, with separate Balance Sheets. Marx then acquires Spengler and the table shows the separate Balance Sheets after the acquisition.

£'000s	M	S		M	S
Share Capital	5	1	Fixed Assets	4	3
Reserves	3	2	Purchase of S. Ltd	3	—
Current Liabilities	2	2	Current Assets	3	2
	£10	5		£10	5

Marx has purchased all the shares of Spengler for £3,000, thus Spengler has become a wholly owned subsidiary of Marx, and consolidated accounts can be prepared for presentation to the shareholders at the year end. The Consolidated Balance Sheet is set out below:

CONSOLIDATED BALANCE SHEET

Share Capital	5	Fixed Assets	7
Reserves	3	Current Assets	5
Current Liabilities	4		
	£12		£12

Fixed Assets – the Fixed Assets of the two companies are added together (M4 + S3 = 7) to provide the Balance Sheet figure.

Current Assets – The Current Assets are added together (M3 + S2 = 5). Added to the Fixed Assets, the Total Assets of the group (£12) are shown.

Current Liabilities – The Current Liabilities of the two companies are added together (M2 + S2 = 4).

Share Capital and Reserves – Marx has purchased all the shares in Spengler, therefore the only shares shown on the consolidated Balance Sheet are those of Marx (£5).

– Marx has bought all the reserves of Spengler in the purchase agreement, so these also are removed from the consolidated Balance Sheet, leaving only the reserves of Marx Ltd (£3).

In adding together the current assets and liabilities, we have assumed that Marx is not a trade creditor or debtor of Spengler, nor Spengler of Marx. Had there been such a relationship, the consolidated figure would have been reduced by the relevant amount, since the consolidated Balance Sheet shows only the links *outside* the group. The same applies in the Profit and Loss Account with sales within the group. This is why the preparation of a consolidated set of accounts is a complex business – intra-group transfers and relationships have to be netted out.

In its purchase for £3,000 of Spengler Ltd, the main company has paid the exact figure necessary to cancel the value of Spengler's share capital (£1,000) and reserves (£2,000). In other words Marx Ltd has paid the Balance Sheet value for the Net Assets of Spengler Ltd – Fixed Assets £3,000 + (Current Assets £2,000 – Current Liabilities £2,000) = £3,000. Had Marx paid £4,000 for Spengler, the accountant would have a problem when consolidating the two Balance Sheets. Marx would be shown as paying £4,000 for Spengler, but only obtaining £3,000 of Net Assets. Such an occurrence is quite common in takeovers and mergers, and accountants handle this problem by calling the difference between what is paid for a subsidiary and the value of its assets, 'goodwill'.

(c) Goodwill

The monetary quantification concept (Chapter 1, Section 1.1(c)) specified that if an item could not be quantified in monetary terms, then it could not be brought into the books of account. So where 'goodwill' appears in a Balance Sheet it means something different from the normal usage of that word.

Goodwill can only arise where a company has been purchased by another company for more than the book value of its assets. It is a figure which includes the normal 'goodwill' of a business but will include other items which do not appear in an accounting Balance Sheet such as:

(i)   management expertise;
(ii) know-how;
(iii) trade names;
(iv) patents.

To make the books balance, the accountant must take the difference between what was paid for the company, and what the Balance Sheet of that company shows, as goodwill, and show it on the asset side of the Group Balance Sheet. Conversely, if the price paid is less than the book value, it is termed 'negative goodwill' ('not bad will').

For example, if Marx had paid £4,000 for Spengler by raising an additional £1,000 from shareholders then the Consolidated Balance Sheet would appear as:

CONSOLIDATED BALANCE SHEET

Share Capital	6	Fixed Assets	7
Reserves	3	Goodwill	1
Current Liabilities	4	Current Assets	5
	£13		£13

(d) Minority interest

Sometimes one of the subsidiaries is not completely owned by the parent company, and there are shareholders other than the parent company. To show the shareholders what really belongs to them in the group accounts, it is necessary to show separately the amount that belongs to shareholders outside the group — the minority or outsider shareholders.

(e) Share Premium Account

If a company issues shares at a price greater than their nominal value (at a premium), the additional amount raised must be shown separately in the 'Share Premium Account', since the only amount of share capital shown in the Balance Sheet is the nominal value of the shares. It is not possible, in the UK, to issue shares at a discount and thereby create the opposite type of account.

(f) Taxation

In the annual accounts of companies taxation appears in both the Profit and Loss Account and the Balance Sheet (see Currys' Accounts in Chapter 2, Section 2.5). The Profit and Loss Account shows the tax charge on the profits for the year, which the company owes to the Government (it may also include adjustments for stock relief, and capital gains tax on asset sales). The basic UK tax is corporation tax (currently 52 per cent). The Balance Sheet will show under Current Liabilities the tax due, and there may be a heading for Deferred Taxation. All 'deferred' means in this context is that payment of that liability has been put off to a future period, that it is not due for payment within the next year.

In general, company taxation and the preparation of tax accounts is a specialist subject, and its particular intricacies cannot be explored here. For further study on the treatment of taxation in company's accounts, SSAP 4 and SSAP 15 should be consulted, and for the tax incentives in Government regional policies, and the tax and cash flow implications (see Chapter 5) of alternative options in particular companies and industries, the Inland Revenue's information leaflets, special books on tax, and specialist advisers should be consulted. This particularly applies to the purchase of land, property, and other major assets, and to lease-or-buy decisions.

3.7 THE ANALYSIS OF PUBLISHED ACCOUNTS

There used to be a bank manager who was well-known for his financial acumen. When a customer brought in a set of accounts he would study the Profit and Loss Account and the Balance Sheet for less than one minute before deciding how much to advance. His record was good, and his reputation as a financial wizard tremendous. When he retired he passed his secret on to his colleagues. If the customer had blue eyes he gave him everything he asked for; if brown, he gave 50 per cent; any other colour received nothing.

We do not know whether he was colour blind, nor how the loans were secured, but the belief that the professional finance man or accountant can pick up a set of accounts and in a matter of seconds take major long-term decisions is a myth. It requires much work, as well as experience, to produce a sensible analysis of a set of accounts. To this task the remainder of this chapter and Chapter 5 are devoted.

In any analysis one must first know what is being sought, and to what end. The principal categories of people who will be interested in the accounts and the questions they will be asking, have already been considered (Chapter 2, Section 2.6). We now investigate the use of measures to assist in answering these questions.

Probably the most common question is whether a company will pay its bills and stay in business. This will be important both to those external to the firm — creditors, bank managers, shareholders — and to the management, who will usually wish to ensure the continued survival of their company and their jobs.

(a) Measures of solvency and liquidity

We have noted the ability of a company to show a healthy profit in its accounts and go bankrupt the following month. Because a company is profitable, this does not mean it has cash resources available. Indeed, it is arguable that control and management of liquid resources is more important than generation of profit. A company can make losses and have ample time to do something about it — several major companies have suffered such situations of several years' losses or very low profits — but any company which finds itself short of cash is in a much more critical situation. Put in simple terms:

$$No\ cash\ = No\ business$$

$$No\ profit = Challenge\ to\ management.$$

In assessing a company's ability to meet short-term liabilities — to pay its current liabilities as they fall due — the relationship between short-term assets and short-term liabilities is vital. The difference is often described as the Working Capital or Net Current Assets of the Company.

$$Current\ Assets - Current\ Liabilities$$

$$= Working\ Capital\ or\ Net\ Current\ Assets$$

A company with positive working capital has more short-term assets than short-term liabilities. There are sufficient funds in current assets to pay all its current liabilities.

Any company which has to pay out its current liabilities might be expected to follow a series of steps:

(i)   Write cheques to the value of its cash holdings;
(ii) Call in cash from customers' credit accounts (creditors);
(iii) Sell inventory on the best possible terms;
(iv) Sell some fixed assets.

Normally only the first two steps will be necessary. Any company which reaches the stage of selling off fixed assets to pay current liabilities is getting past redemption.

From the above, a company which has positive working capital might seem comparatively safe in terms of its ability to pay short-term debts; conversely, a company with negative working capital (more Current Liabilities than Current Assets) might seem unsafe. But unfortunately financial analysis is not as simple as that. Much will depend upon the kind of markets the company operates in, the stage of development reached by the company, its relationship with bankers and other financial sources, and the time of year at which the Balance Sheet has been prepared. For example the most recent figures for Marks and Spencer Ltd show:

31 March, £m	1977	1978	1979
Current Liabilities	125	182	241
Current Assets	118	174	232
Negative Working Capital	7	8	9

The company has had a negative working capital position over these three years' accounts, yet it is a very healthy trading company. Had the Balance Sheet been made up at a different time of year a quite different situation might have appeared in the company's working capital. Alternatively the size of current liabilities may show that the company can get good credit terms (nearly two months) from its suppliers. Furthermore with UK sales in 1979 of £1,431.7m mainly for cash over the counter from customers, the company has a very sound basic cashflow which would be the envy of most manufacturing companies.

(b) Liquidity ratios

For assessing the short-term financial viability of companies from their Annual Accounts some simple ratios can be used. We illustrate the application of ratio analysis with five companies, three in civil engineering and construction (Mitchell, Laing and Costain) and two retailers (Marks & Spencer and British Home Stores). For reasons that will soon become clear, figures for 1971 are used.

The *Current Ratio* is a better way of showing the working capital situation, dividing Current Assets by Current Liabilities.

1971 £m	Mitchell	Laing	Costain	M & S	BHS
Current Liabilities	14.4	17.9	25.8	60.9	11.6
Current Assets	17.4	30.5	31.6	66.4	19.2
Working Capital	3.0	12.6	5.8	5.5	7.6
Current Ratio	1.2:1	1.7:1	1.2:1	1.1:1	1.6:1

All of these companies have a current ratio of at least 1:1. For every pound owed short-term in Current Liabilities, there is at least a pound available from Current Assets.

The difficulties associated with valuation of stock were discussed above (Section 3.4). If a strict appraisal of solvency is required, it is best to leave stock out of the current assets, and consider only the liquid assets. If a company had to realise its stock quickly, it would probably not even recover its cost (particularly for work in progress). The ratio then becomes

$$\frac{\text{Current assets} - \text{Stock}}{\text{Current Liabilities}}$$

and for the five companies the ratio is:

Mitchell	Laing	Costain	M & S	BHS
0.3:1	1:1	0.9:1	0.6:1	0.9:1

Mitchell appears the weakest under this second ratio — sometimes termed the *'acid test'*. This means that if the company were forced to pay its current liabilities quickly, and the investment in stocks and work-in-progress could not be turned into cash in time, then the company would not be able to pay in full without recourse to borrowing.

The ideal ratio should be at least 1:1. But, again, there are no universal standards and the various particular factors must be considered in assessing a company's acceptability under this ratio. There is danger in having too good an acid-test ratio, for the company might become an attractive proposition to companies which could use such liquid assets. Too high a ratio might also indicate that the company is not making adequate use of its finances: cash by itself does not generate much profit.

Another ratio which can usefully be employed in this analysis is the *current liquidity ratio*:

$$\frac{\text{Current liabilities} - (\text{Current assets} - \text{Stock})}{\text{Profit before tax and interest}} \times 365$$

For the five companies this ratio is:

	Mitchell	*Laing*	*Costain*	*M & S*	*BHS*
Number of days	2,864	−37	235	176	51

Mitchell again comes out weakest. This ratio shows that it would take Mitchell 2,864 days (almost eight years), working at the profit level of 1971, to pay off the deficit between current liabilities and liquid assets. Laing is so liquid that it has a negative figure for 1971.

These ratios are indicators of solvency and liquidity, and do not in themselves cause insolvency or cash problems. They can act as warnings that a company is in a precarious situation. Mitchell went into liquidation in January 1973, yet had been operating successfully in previous years on similar ratios. All that could be said on the basis of these ratios is that if anything happened to slow the flow of funds into Mitchell there was little cushion there.

The importance of relating the ratio to the particular firm and industry cannot be overstressed. Little is gained from comparing Costain with BHS − who happened to have the same 0.9:1 acid test ratio in 1971. It is more realistic to compare BHS with M & S, as they are in the same business. In the ratios used so far, BHS appears more liquid than M & S. The companies had different approaches to financial management.

(c) Profitability measures
The most common ratio used for measuring profitability is *return on capital employed* (ROCE):

$$\text{ROCE} = \frac{\text{Profit}}{\text{Capital employed}} \times 100$$

As this is the most commonly used, it also tends to be the most commonly misused. Before comparing ROCEs all the terms in the calculation must be clearly defined. What sort of profit is being used? Pre-tax, post-tax, before interest, after depreciation, or what? And how is capital employed calculated: total assets, net assets or some other basis? In this book the definition of 'capital employed' is:

Fixed assets + Current assets − Current liabilities

Using four companies' 1979 accounts (M & S, Tesco, Currys and Pilkington) the pre- and post-tax profits related to capital employed are as follows:

	M & S	Tesco	Currys	Pilkington
Pre-tax ROCE	30%	20%	23%	16%
Post-tax ROCE	16%	20%	16%	9% .

This ratio shows the profit generated on the capital employed in the company and can be a useful measure of efficiency. There are problems with its application, in that the fixed assets are taken at the Balance Sheet valuation, and the valuation method may differ between companies. Ideally for comparison all the assets in the companies should be valued in the same manner. Furthermore a company may not own many fixed assets, because it rents or leases them. This can distort the comparison as well.

Comparing the ROCE in retailing with that in manufacturing (as represented by Pilkington), the ROCE of the manufacturing business is lower than that of the retailers. This is partly because retailers do not have the vast manufacturing investment required by Pilkington, and partly because profit levels in the industries differ. This can be illustrated by looking at the relationship of sales income to the other factors involved.

Sales help to generate the total profit, which is the mark-up or profit margin times unit sales. The relationship between sales and capital employed is measured by the *asset turnover ratio*. This shows how many times each year the assets are turned over by the sales generated through their use. Many companies use an extension of this concept in the Du Pont chart (named after the company which first produced this schema in the 1950s). This chart expresses the Profit and Loss Account in the single ratio of profit to sales. The Balance Sheet is also reduced to a single ratio, the number of times each year the sales cover (or turn over) the capital employed. An example of a Du Pont chart is shown in Fig. 3.1.

If the profit percentage and the asset turnover are multiplied together, the resulting percentage is the ROCE. The two ratios are:

$$\frac{\text{Profit}}{\text{Sales}} \times \frac{\text{Sales}}{\text{Capital employed}}$$

Sales cancel out, leaving:

$$\frac{\text{Profit}}{\text{Capital employed}}$$

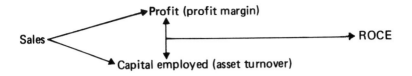

Fig. 3.1 *An example of the Du Pont chart*

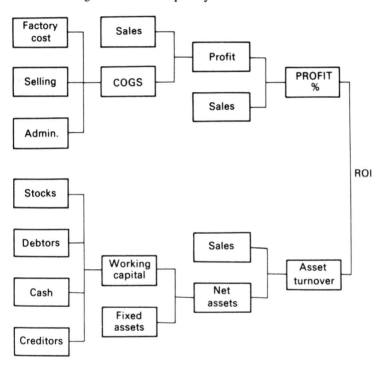

Showing ROCE in a Du Pont chart highlights its value as a profit measure, for ROCE combines the profit made on sales with the capital used to produce those sales.

The ratios for the three retailing firms and Pilkington for 1979 are:

	M & S	Tesco	Currys	Pilkington
Profit margin	11%	3%	6%	16%
Asset turnover	2.8	6.5	3.8	1.0
Pre-tax ROCE	30%	20%	23%	16%

From these two component ratios of the ROCE calculation, we can assess the overall profit margin and the use made of the investment in the company (capital employed) to generate the sales revenue from which this profit margin is derived. On this evidence alone, it becomes clear that M & S and Tesco have different strategies. M & S goes for a relatively high profit margin and low asset turnover; Tesco are in a low-margin, high-volume business, suggesting they are in a price-sensitive sector. The manufacturing firm of Pilkington is notably different, with a high profit margin but low asset turnover. It is always worth analysing these ratios over a number of years to discover whether there is consistency over time, or whether the way in which a company achieves its return on capital is changing.

(d) ROCE and revaluation

As ROCE is widely used for assessing company performance, managements usually give it close attention. If a company revalues its assets this automatically reduces the ROCE percentage. This is one of the reasons why companies may not favour an asset revaluation. Indeed, it can be argued that a board of directors should only revalue the company's assets on two occasions. First, where a takeover is threatened, so that the purchasing company is forced to pay for the value of the assets, and second, where the company wishes to borrow more money on the strength of the assets shown in the Balance Sheet. To revalue at any other time may show an adverse picture of the directors' activities, unless one judges the directors to be partly responsible for the increase in the assets' values. On these issues the interests of directors and shareholders may diverge, so any investor would be wise to pay attention to market values rather than book values. Such attention is usually reflected, of course, in the price of the shares in the case of a quoted company.

(e) Other working capital measures

There are several other ratios which can be helpful in assessing the performance and financial management of a company. Stock is part of the capital employed in the business, for the company has used some of its funds to build up stock. If the company holds excessive stock it may be locking up financial resources in an unused and possibly depreciating asset, or it may be hedging against price inflation. Certainly, if the company holds too little stock it may lose sales revenue and profit through not being able to service its customers. To measure how much is tied up in stock, and how quickly the stock is turned over, two ratios can be used:

$$\frac{\text{Stock}}{\text{Current assets}} \quad \text{and} \quad \frac{\text{Sales}}{\text{Stock}}$$

The first of these shows what proportion of the current assets is held in stock, and the second shows how many times during the year the stock is turned over by the sales. For the four companies these ratios are:

	M & S	Tesco	Currys	Pilkington
Stock as a percentage of current assets	41%	80%	48%	33%
Stock turnover	15	9	6	5

The two that stand out are Tesco with a high proportion of current assets held in stock, and Pilkington with a low stock turnover. On the whole, the greater the stock turnover figure, the better, for if the goods are being sold at a profit, then the more sold the greater the profit at the year end (assuming a fixed pricing policy).

In most business after a sale has occurred there is usually a delay before payment is received. This credit period can be used to assess how well management is speeding the flow of cash through the business. The ratio is calculated as:

$$\frac{\text{Debtors}}{\text{Average daily sales}}$$

For Pilkington the figure is 82 days for 1979 compared with 77 days in 1978. In using this ratio the nature of the particular business must be taken into account. Basic manufacturing business such as Pilkington with export business to finance is obliged to grant much longer credit than the UK retailing operations represented by the other three companies.

Debtors can also be used to assess the overall soundness of the company's short-term financial situation, by comparing this figure with creditors in the ratio:

$$\frac{\text{Debtors}}{\text{Creditors}}$$

If a trend is observed where creditors begin to outweigh debtors, this can be a sign of overtrading. The company is stretching itself too far, selling more goods than it can finance, and failing to collect the revenues. A short-term solution is to call in cash as quickly as possible from debtors, and make creditors wait as long as possible before payment. But this may be taken as a sign of financial difficulty, further complicating relations with suppliers and customers. In both consumer and industrial markets credit is part of the marketing package, depending on particular company and industry practice. In times of high interest rates for instance, small suppliers often have to give long credit to major customers — apparently good financial management by the dominant trading partner, but the cost is borne by the weaker.

(f) Conclusion

The reader is now recommended to obtain a set of published accounts, and try to analyse and understand them. This is the best test of this chapter's efficacy.

4 Inflation Accounting

In the first three chapters of this book the basic principles of financial accounting have been introduced, and the practical problems generated by inflation largely ignored. These are now considered.

4.1 THE INFLATION PROBLEM

In times of inflation the prices of consumer goods generally are rising, usually reflecting rising prices for materials, commodities and other factors of production. To some extent price rises in the former can be offset by changes in the pattern of consumption, and price rises in the latter by increases in productivity, by technological advances, by switches between productive inputs, perhaps by economies of scale. Witness, for example, the drastic decreases in the retail prices of ballpoint pens from the 1950s to 1960s; the massive decrease in the costs of computing power, of calculators, digital watches and other electronic goods in the last decade. These decreases have occurred against a general background of increases in the price of goods that make up the Retail Price Index (RPI), a basket of consumer commodities which is used as the benchmark measure of inflation in the UK. Since this is a general measure, it will be clear that different individuals, industries and companies will be affected in different ways by the inflation in the RPI. There may even be a deflation in some factors of production (and so, in competitive markets, in some selling prices), as occurred with the development of plastics for a wide range of industrial uses, though plastic has suffered subsequently from the enormous increases in oil prices. Inflation (particularly when unanticipated) tends to favour debtors and those whose income can increase with prices, at the expense of creditors and those on fixed incomes. For instance, the face value of a mortgage on a £10,000 house bought ten years ago will be unchanged, but the market value of the property will have more than doubled while the average annual interest payments will have increased to a relatively small degree.

How does inflation affect financial reporting? Under inflation one of the key concepts of financial accounting, the use of cost as a basis for valuation, is called into question. For many years it was realistic for the accountant to assume that the measure (whether pound, dollar, drachma or cowrie shell) used in preparing the accounts of a company remained of constant value from year to year. This made it possible to compare one year's accounts with another and undertake comparative analysis. But when the monetary unit becomes elastic, when the 1978 pound does not have similar purchasing power to the 1979 pound, then it becomes difficult to compare company performance between these years, and fundamental flaws appear in the accounting derivation of profit.

Two simple examples will illustrate the problems. Take the case of a driver who decides in 1975 to set himself up in business by investing £5,000 in a van and hiring it out with his services. He pays himself wages, covers the van's running costs and, after allowing for straight-line depreciation of the cost of the van in five equal annual amounts, he produces £1,000 retained profit each year. So his 1980 Balance Sheet will appear as:

	Cost	Depreciation	
Fixed Assets			
Van	5,000	5,000	——
Current Assets			
Cash			10,000
			£10,000
Capital			
Initial input	5,000		
Profit	5,000		10,000
			£10,000

The £10,000 appearing as cash is the result of five years' depreciation at £1,000 per year plus five years' retained profits at £1,000 per year. The 1980 Balance Sheet suggests that the driver has doubled his investment over the five-year period. But when he comes to replace the van, he finds that an identical replacement will cost £10,000. Prices have doubled under inflation, and upon replacement of his van the Balance Sheet becomes:

	Cost	Depreciation	
Fixed Assets			
Van	10,000	—	10,000
			£10,000

Capital

Initial input	5,000	
Profit	5,000	10,000
		£10,000

This may appear perfectly satisfactory, with the size of the business double that in 1975. But is this really the case? Has the driver really made the £5,000 profit shown in his Balance Sheet? Is it not more accurate to say that he is in exactly the same position in 1980 after replacement of his van as he was in at the beginning of 1975? In 1975 he had one van and no cash, and in 1980 he has one van and no cash. Due to the impact of inflation he has merely managed to hold steady the size of his business. He is five years older, has managed to survive, and has the scrap value of his old van to show for five years' effort.

As a second example, take a manufacturer with a Profit and Loss Account which shows:

		£
Sales		100,000
Opening stock at cost	20,000	
Purchases at cost	80,000	
	100,000	
Closing stock at cost	50,000	
	Cost of goods sold	50,000
	Gross profit	50,000

He may be pleased with his year's business. But what if the £50,000 closing stock is, in physical terms, exactly the same as his opening stock of £20,000 and the £30,000 difference is the result of inflationary increases in its cost? If the closing stock is worth £50,000 now, then the replacement cost of goods sold would be worth at least £80,000 (the opening stock, now worth £50,000, plus at least £30,000 worth of the year's purchases which have been used in manufacture). Under this reckoning, the profit is £20,000. Has he really made £50,000 gross profit? The answer must be no. Of this profit 60 per cent is due to inflation in stock values, and if after covering overheads he were to take out the net profit as dividend there would be problems later when the stock has to be replaced at the inflated costs. Of course, in compensation, the value of the Rolls Royce he bought with the dividend (he had no tax accountant) will have risen even faster than the cost of replacement stocks.

These two simplified examples illustrate the problems with historic cost accounting conventions in times of inflation. First, the value placed on fixed assets tends to be lower than their real value, and depreciation, charged in the Accounts on historic cost, is insufficient to cover their replacement. Second, where a company is producing and selling a product, 'stock profits' can arise, which produce an overstatement of profitability. If the 'profit' is distributed there may be insufficient finance for the increased working capital requirements. Third, in times of inflation it can be difficult to gauge the real growth of a business in terms of sales or profitability if there is no adjustment for the decrease in purchasing power of the monetary unit used in the accounts. It is problems such as these that have prompted consideration of alternative ways of presenting financial information under conditions of inflation.

4.2 THE BACKGROUND TO INFLATION ACCOUNTING PROPOSALS

The problem of presenting meaningful financial information during conditions of inflation has long been recognised by the accounting profession. In May 1952 the ICAEW discussed the limitations of historic cost accounting in conditions of inflation:

> ... the monetary cost at which stock-in-trade is charged against revenue is not sufficient during a period of rising prices, to meet the cost of replacing the same quantity of stock; and similarly depreciation charges based on the monetary cost of fixed assets will not provide the amount required to meet the cost of replacement of those assets at higher prices if and when they need to be replaced. Monetary profits do not therefore necessarily reflect an increase or decrease in wealth in terms of purchasing power; and in times of material change in prices this limitation upon the significance of monetary profits may be very important . . . . . nor do the results necessarily represent the amount which can prudently be regarded as available for distribution, having regard to the financial requirements of the business. Similarly the results shown by such accounts are not necessarily suitable for purposes such as price fixing, wage negotiations and taxation . . . [1]

Price fixing may not be quite the right word, but this Statement of Accounting Principles also stated:

> It would be a major development in the building of a coherent and logical structure of accounting principles if the limitations of accounts based on historical cost could be eliminated or reduced by the adoption of new principles, capable of practical application to all kinds of businesses in a manner which would be independent of personal opinion

to a degree comparable with the existing principles based on historic cost.

Some twenty-five years later this 'major development' has not yet been achieved. But the accounting profession has taken steps towards a set of principles relating to inflation accounting. In January 1973 the Accounting Standards Committee issued an exposure draft (ED 8)[2] which was eventually translated into a provisional standard (SSAP 7) in May 1974. The proposal was that the impact of inflation on companies' financial figures should be tackled by adjusting key figures in the accounts on the basis of changes in the index of retail prices (RPI) since, it was argued, changes in the RPI represented overall changes in the purchasing power of money. The operation of this proposal was termed Current Purchasing Power Accounting (CPP). Though the application of RPI adjustments to accounts in general has been rejected, the mechanics of adjustment remain valid to any attempt to adjust accounts for inflation.

To illustrate the process, suppose a house is purchased by a developer in 1975 for £20,000, and sold in 1980 for £40,000. What profit or gain has been realised? If there had been no inflation during the period 1975–80 then there would be a gain of £20,000. Under inflation the true profit would be lower than £20,000. With an index which measures inflation in the housing market it is possible to assess the inflationary profit element. Suppose that when the asset was purchased the index was 100, and when sold, the index was 160. We can now apply the change in the index to the cost of the asset:

$$\text{Historic Cost} \times \frac{\text{Index Today}}{\text{Index at Date of Purchase}}$$

$$£20,000 \times \frac{160}{100} = £32,000$$

The historic cost of the asset (£20,000) has been translated into a more realistic current value of £32,000. So, in this simplified example, the £20,000 apparent profit consists of £12,000 inflation profit and £8,000 true profit. This method of adjustment through the use of relevant index numbers has direct application in inflation accounting. Under CPP Accounting the asset would have its value adjusted by changes in the RPI, and the resulting figure would be termed its CPP value. However, the general use of RPI adjustments for all types of company accounts was subject to severe criticism, and SSAP 7 was not widely applied by companies in their annual accounts.

In 1973 the Government set up the Sandilands Committee to consider inflation accounting. The Committee first met in January 1974, and reported in September 1975.[3] It rejected CPP accounting and the application of the RPI to all companies as unrealistic, and recommended the adoption of a system of Current Cost Accounting (CCA):

> We have reached three main conclusions. First, we consider that it is essential that accounts should allow for changes in costs and prices. Secondly, we consider that existing accounting conventions do not do so adequately, and tend to present the affairs of companies in a misleading way . . . . Thirdly, while acknowledging the valuable contribution to the subject made by the issue of Exposure Draft 8 and SSAP 7 we consider that the most fruitful line of development in inflation accounting is a system based on the principles of value accounting, which shows the specific impact of inflation on the individual companies. We recommend that a system to be known as Current Cost Accounting should be developed. . . .
>
> (Paragraphs 10 and 11)

The Sandilands Committee concentrated on the two main issues facing financial accounting under conditions of changing prices – valuation and profit measurement. After consideration of various methods of valuation, it was recommended that:

> . . . as far as possible a balance sheet should show the value to the business of a company's assets . . . . The value to the business of an asset is to be equated with the amount of the loss suffered by the company concerned if the asset is lost or destroyed.
>
> (Paragraphs 527 and 529)

Generally the 'value to the business' of an asset will be its written-down current replacement cost. This net replacement cost (NRC) is the amount needed to replace the asset with an identical asset of the same age. In most cases the value to the business for Fixed Assets can be calculated by adjusting the historic cost valuation with an appropriate index of price movements, using the same mechanical process as described above.

In considering measures of profitability Sandilands recommended that the total profit or gain should be divided into 'realised' and 'unrealised' elements and:

> Operating Gains – the profit made from carrying on the particular business of the company
>
> Extraordinary Gains – profits arising from other than the mainstream activities of the company

Holding Gains — gains arising from increases in the value of assets held by the company.

To illustrate, suppose a company purchases goods for £1,000, and after an interval sells them for £2,000. If there were no inflation, there would be an accounting profit of £1,000. However, under price inflation in the market for these goods, shown by an index which was 100 when the goods were purchased and 150 when sold, a different calculation is required to provide a statement of current operating profit.

		£
Revenue		2,000
Value to the business of goods consumed or disposed of	$1,000 \times \dfrac{150}{100}$	1,500
Current Cost Operating Profit		£ 500

The current cost operating profit is £500, and there is a realised holding gain of £500, making up the conventional accounting profit of £1,000. The current cost operating profit (COP) is calculated after charging the 'value to the business' of the goods — their replacement cost — and the holding gain arises because the assets have increased in value due to price changes over time. If the conventional historic cost accounting profit of £1,000 were taken, this would produce an overstatement of real profitability since replacement of the stock will require £1,500 (not the original £1,000). This underlines a key aspect of inflation accounting, the attempt *to provide for the maintenance of the operating capability of the company.*

The Sandilands Committee recommended that Current Cost Accounting should be the subject of an accounting standard (an SSAP) as soon as possible. An Inflation Accounting Steering Group (IASG) was set up to supervise this, with Douglas Morpeth as Chairman. In 1976 it issued ED 18 together with a 'Guidance Manual' on CCA.

4.3 THE CURRENT POSITION

From 1976 to 1978 there was continuing debate on different possible approaches to practical inflation accounting, and on the introduction of CCA. The profession rejected compulsory introduction of the recommendations in ED 18 as too complex, untried, and failing to cover all aspects of the impact of inflation on a company. One might think the first and third objections are inconsistent. But following this, a subcommittee of ASC was set up, under the chairmanship of Michael Hyde, which published the 'Hyde Guidelines' in November 1977. An example of the type of statement recommended by Hyde is shown in the CCA Statement of Currys, reproduced as Fig. 4.1.

On 30 April 1979, ED 24 was issued to provide the basis for an accounting standard on CCA (and SSAP 16 was subsequently issued in March 1980) with the aim of reflecting 'the impact of specific price changes on the business when: (a) determining profits for an accounting period; and (b) preparing the balance sheet' (para. 24). The intention is that this accounting standard will apply to all quoted companies and others with a

---

Fig. 4.1

Currys Limited

Current Cost Accounts

Consolidated Current Cost Statement of Profit and Loss
Year ended 24th January, 1979

	Note (p. 19)	1979 £'000		1978 £'000
Trading profit			10,885	9,218
Less: Adjustments:				
Additional depreciation	(b)	1,045		1,024
Cost of sales	(c)	2,256		2,279
			3,301	3,303
Current cost trading profit			7,584	5,915
Interest receivable less payable			960	529
			8,544	6,444
Add: Gearing adjustment	(d)		22	68
			8,566	6,512
Surplus on sale of properties		603		571
Less: Adjustment to current cost		471		183
			132	388
			8,698	6,900
Depreciation of buildings			804	429
Adjusted profit before taxation			7,894	6,471
Taxation	(e)		4,113	4,911
Adjusted profit available after taxation			3,781	1,560

Fig. 4.1 *continued*

Consolidated Balance Sheets
24th January, 1979

	Current Cost Accounts		Historical Cost Accounts	
	1979 £'000	1978 £'000	1979 £'000	1978 £'000
Land and buildings	51,336	36,457	14,975	14,401
Other fixed assets	6,362	5,570	5,039	4,116
Total fixed assets	57,698	42,027	20,014	18,517
A.C.T. recoverable	474	560	474	560
Current assets less current liabilities	29,637	24,188	29,637	24,188
Net assets	87,809	66,775	50,125	43,265
Less: Preference shares	660	660	660	660
Total equity interest	87,149	66,115	49,465	42,605
Represented by:				
Ordinary share capital	5,822	5,822	5,822	5,822
Revaluation/Inflation reserve	55,357	37,433	17,673	13,923
General reserves	25,970	22,860	25,970	22,860
	87,149	66,115	49,465	42,605
Assets per share	374.2p	283.9p	212.4p	183.0p

Notes to the current cost accounts

a) The consolidated current cost statement of profit and loss has been prepared in accordance with the interim recommendation on inflation accounting issued on 4th November, 1977 by the Accounting Standards Committee.

b) Fixed assets have been restated at their present value to the business. The following bases have been used:

Land and buildings—In consultation with professional advisers the Directors have carried out a full revaluation of properties and the figure arrived at has been used in the current cost accounts. Amortisation of leaseholds and depreciation of buildings has been based on the revaluation figures.

Other fixed assets—These have been revalued at gross current replacement cost calculated by reference to appropriate indices issued by the Central Statistical Office, less aggregate depreciation at the existing rates of depreciation used by the Group.

c) The cost of sales adjustment has been made to charge against profits the replacement cost instead of the historical cost of stocks consumed. In the absence of more relevant trade indices the retail price index has

---

Fig. 4.1 *continued*

been used (r.p.i. January, 1979 207.2, January, 1978 189.5, increase 9.3%).
d) The gearing adjustment eliminates the proportion of the cost of sales and depreciation adjustments financed by net monetary liabilities. The proportion has been calculated by dividing net monetary liabilities by the aggregate of shareholders' interests and net monetary liabilities and applying the resulting fraction to the adjustment.
e) Taxation is charged on the same basis as in the historical cost accounts.

---

turnover of over £5,000,000, becoming operational in 1980. It therefore covers some 5,000 companies.

ED 24 expands the information presented in Currys' CCA Statement to provide a clearer view of the impact of price changes on a company's operations and value. The Profit and Loss Account will show the current cost operating profit (COP) by making a series of adjustments to the profit shown by conventional accounting:

(i) *Depreciation Adjustment* – to arrive at COP the 'value to the business' of the assets consumed during the year must be charged in the Profit and Loss Account. This will usually result in a higher depreciation charge than used in conventional accounts, with the fixed assets either revalued or having their values adjusted on the basis of indices upon which 'value to the business' depreciation is calculated.

This can be seen in Currys' CCA Statement, which shows additional depreciation charges of £1.045m, and £0.804m.

(ii) *Cost of Sales Adjustment* – the conventional Profit and Loss Account has the cost of goods consumed as a charge. If the prices of these goods have been changing during the year, an adjustment must be made to ensure that the 'value to the business' of goods consumed during the year is applied. Normally this can be done by using the replacement cost of goods consumed and an average of the index.

Note (c) describes how the retail price index has been used in the calculation of Currys' cost of sales adjustment of £2.256m. Obviously there will be different indices for different industries, and the Central Statistical

Office publishes 'Price Index Numbers for Current Cost Accounting'[4] to assist in this.

For applying the changes in a price index to the figures in conventional accounts to produce the Cost of Sales Adjustment (COSA), one takes the index at the beginning and end of the financial year and the average index for the year (e.g. the index over twelve months divided by twelve). These figures are then used to provide an adjustment that will approximate to a charge for the replacement cost of stock to be made in arriving at the COP. For example:

Opening stock	£10,000	
Closing stock	£15,000	
Relevant Index — when opening stock acquired	220	
when closing stock acquired	280	
average for the year	260	

Stock change in conventional accounts £15,000 − £10,000 = £5,000
Less

$$£15,000 \times \frac{260}{280} - £10,000 \times \frac{260}{220}$$

£13,929	− £11,818	= £2,111
	Cost of Sales Adjustment	£2,889

(iii) *Monetary Working Capital Adjustment* — the net operating assets of a company include not only the fixed assets and stock, but also working capital. Adequate working capital is required to continue in business, and price changes are as important here as elsewhere. Monetary working capital is, in most cases, the difference between debtors and creditors as shown in the balance sheets. To show the impact of price changes on monetary working capital a calculation similar to that for the cost of sales adjustment is made. An average of the relevant index is used to adjust the figures appearing in the conventional accounts.

Currys' CCA Statement does not include this monetary working capital adjustment (MWCA) since this has only been introduced with the publication of SSAP 16, applying from 1 January 1980.

The Current Cost Profit and Loss Account, so far, appears as:

	£'000s
Turnover for year	
Historic Cost Operating Profit	–
Current Cost Adjustments	
Depreciation	
Cost of Sales	
Monetary Working Capital	–
Current Cost Operating Profit	£ –

The COP shown here is the total profit generated by the company in the year. In order to show the profit relating to the capital provided by ordinary shareholders, one further adjustment must be made:

(iv) *Gearing Adjustment* – where capital is provided by sources other than shareholders there will be a benefit to shareholders as the impact of inflation erodes the face value of the company's borrowing. Thus if the company borrowed £1,000 in 1975 at a fixed rate of interest, and repays the loan in 1980, it will be repaying in 1980 pounds which, due to inflation, are not the same as 1975 pounds. The gearing adjustment reduces the impact of the other adjustments according to the proportion of external borrowing.

Currys' CCA Statement shows a gearing adjustment of £22,000 and the method of calculation is explained in their Note (d).
The form for the Current Cost Profit and Loss Account is:

	£'000
Turnover	
Historic Cost Operating Profit	–
Current Cost Adjustments	
Depreciation	
Cost of Sales	
Monetary Working Capital	–
Current Cost Operating Profit	£ –
Gearing Adjustment	–
Interest	–
Current Cost Profit before taxation	£ –
Taxation	–

Current Cost Profit attributable to shareholders	−
Dividends	−
Retained Current Cost Profit for the year	£ −
Current Cost Earnings per share	£ −

Thus the Current Cost Profit and Loss Account follows the normal form of presentation adopted in a conventional Profit and Loss Account, but current cost data is used throughout.

Under SSAP 16, companies will also be providing a Current Cost Balance Sheet similar to the one shown in Currys' CCA Statement. There will be a Capital Maintenance Reserve shown which will reflect all the current cost adjustments as well as any revaluation surpluses or deficits. The Current Cost Balance Sheet will appear as:

Assets Employed		
Fixed Assets		£'000s
Net Current Assets		
Stock	−	
Debtors less Creditors	−	
Other Current Liabilities	−	−
Financed By		
Capital and Reserves		
Issued Share Capital	−	
Capital Maintenance Reserve	−	
Retained Profit	−	
Loan Capital		−
		£ −

The form of the current cost balance sheet is slightly different to that in the conventional accounts, but the presentation is consistent with the information in the historic cost balance sheet.

Conclusion

All assets and liabilities whose valuation depends on a monetary denomination (cash, debtors, creditors, loans etc.) will lose value in time of inflation. Non-monetary assets (materials, stocks, capital equipment, buildings, land) will change in value depending on the price movements in their relevant markets, and the wear and tear on them. The adjustments recommended in SSAP 16 attempt to account for the effects of these changes in values of both monetary and non-monetary items. The new CCA Standard provides companies with the option of adopting Current Cost Accounting for the Statutory accounts prepared under the Companies Acts, but key sections of historic cost accounts must still appear elsewhere in the Annual Report.

While considerable steps have been taken towards improving corporate reporting under conditions of inflation, it is not certain that a comprehensive practical solution has been achieved. Henry Gold, Head of Accounting Research in the Royal Dutch/Shell Group, writing on SSAP 16 in *The Accountant's Magazine*[5] stated:

> ... the controversy and doubts which have dogged previous attempts to reach a conclusion will continue. Most obviously the Standard is more extensive and therefore potentially more troublesome in its effects on financial reporting than any others. There is also a background of much less experience than is usually the case with a standardised accounting practice .... And so, with SSAP 16, the wheel turns. There should be no illusions about it having come to final rest.

5 Financial Planning

Chapter 3 examined some of the financial ratios used in the analysis of published accounts. These ratios may be used by both insiders and outsiders to help answer such questions as: Can the company pay its debts? What is its profitability and growth record? How does it compare with other firms in the industry? The published Profit and Loss Account and Balance Sheet can be supplemented with information from the reports and ancillary statements contained in the Annual Report.

For example, in the 1979 Annual Report of Marks and Spencer Ltd it is possible to build on the Profit and Loss Account with information from the notes, the Directors' Report and the Chairman's Statement:

Turnover for 1979	£	
UK – Clothing and other merchandise	930,891,000	
Foods	429,710,000	1,360,601,000
Europe – Clothing etc.	20,774,000	
Foods	2,801,000	23,575,000
Canada – Clothing etc.	58,250,000	
Foods	5,045,000	63,295,000
Exports		25,483,000
Total turnover for the year		£1,472,954,000

Expenses for 1979	£
Depreciation	13,333,000
Repairs and Maintenance	10,621,000
Plant hire	800,000
Interest payments	9,979,000
Employees' profit sharing scheme	2,695,000
Directors' emoluments	1,089,000
Employees' remuneration	105,683,000

82

Other useful data
    Average number of employees   43,963
    Total square footage in operation in UK   4,267,000

Details of the auditor's remuneration, charitable donations and other items can also be discovered.

Nevertheless, it is not possible from the Accounts to discover the comparative profitability of food sales against clothing sales or to answer such questions as how M & S manages to make such a good, and continued, profit.

Some of the above data can be used to make comparisons between the firms used in Chapter 3 (based on 1977 accounts, in £'000):

	M & S	*Tesco*	*Currys*
Profit per employee	£4	£1	£2
Sales per employee	£33	£26	£29

These figures can form the basis for a discussion of the comparative success of the management of these companies, but other factors would have to be considered in assessing performance. For example, Tesco has the largest number of stores, but they tend to be smaller than those of M & S, and the companies are not direct competitors.

On the other hand, a manager working in a company will usually be able to get information on most aspects of operations, and make use of this information to analyse past and forecast future results. But before the use of ratios as predictors is considered, a final tool for the analysis of published accounts must be covered — funds flow analysis. This will also be used in financial forecasting and planning.

5.1 FUNDS FLOW ANALYSIS

The annual Balance Sheet of a company shows the assets and liabilities at the year end. The operations will have produced a flow of funds throughout the year, and the assets and liabilities will have been changing throughout the year, particularly in the area of working capital. The term 'funds' is used, in preference to 'cash', because many such changes will not be in strict cash terms, but relate to items such as debtors and creditors which are not necessarily cash items at the time of analysis. The profit shown in the Profit and Loss Account, for instance, which will normally be one of the main sources of funds to a company, is not a 'cash' prcfit, as discussed under the concept of accrual in Chapter 1.

The flow of financial resources can be followed through the changes in two consecutive Balance Sheets. Using Currys' Balance Sheets for 1978 and 1979 (shown in Chapter 2, Section 2.5) one can discover which figures have changed over the twelve-month period separating the Balance Sheets. The 1978 figures are deducted from those of 1979 and the change shown as either an increase or a decrease, as follows:

	£'000s	
	Increase	Decrease
Fixed Assets	1,497	
Advanced Corporation Tax		86
Current Assets	7,023	
Current Liabilities	1,574	
Shareholders' Funds	6,860	

For each net change, one question has to be answered: is it a source or a use of funds? Or, to put the question another way, has the change resulted from a use of 'cash' or from the receipt of 'cash'? Cash is placed in inverted commas because, as noted above, the Balance Sheet items are not necessarily reflected in real cash, but may be the right to receive cash in the future, or the obligation to pay it out in the future.

For example, in the Currys' case, the increase in Fixed Assets of £1,497,000 is a net use of funds by the company, an investment of financial resources in physical assets. The increase of £6,860,000 in Shareholders' Funds is a source of funds to the company from the retention of the year's profits. The increase in Current Assets is a use of funds (£7,023,000), while the increase of £1,574,000 in Current Liabilities represents a source of funds, in effect additional short-term borrowing. The decrease in Advance Corporation Tax (£86,000) also acts as a source of funds: an asset has been reduced, and the funds tied up in that asset freed for use within the business. These changes can be set out as follows:

Sources of Funds	£'000s	
Decrease in Advance Corporation Tax	86	
Increase in Current Liabilities	1,574	
Increase in Shareholders' Funds	6,860	£8,520
Uses of Funds		
Increase in Fixed Assets	1,497	
Increase in Current Assets	7,023	£8,520

If the original Balance Sheets balanced, and the sums have been done accurately, then the Funds Flow Statement must also balance. The *sources of funds must exactly equal the uses of funds* if the rules of book-keeping are maintained.

But this analysis for Currys does not tell us very much. What is required is a more detailed and realistic Funds Flow Statement. But why is it worth the effort?

The ratios discussed in Chapter 2 are a basis for assessing a company's financial state on the evidence of the Balance Sheet, comparing current with past ratios. Is there a trend developing? What does it show? The focus is on changes over time. This is where funds flow analysis helps – it concentrates on changes, ignoring anything that has not moved since the previous Balance Sheet. Funds flow analysis pre-digests the Balance Sheet and shows what has changed. Where have the financial resources of the company been generated, and how have they been used? If a five-year Funds Flow Statement is prepared for a company, its financial management can be assessed more easily than if five years' Balance Sheets were studied.

For a full appreciation, each item on the Balance Sheet must be considered in some detail. The Funds Flow Statement provided above for Currys Ltd is not detailed enough. In preparing a full Funds Flow Statement some simple rules can be followed:

  (i) Increases in assets are uses of funds;
 (ii) Decreases in assets are sources of funds;
(iii) Increases in liabilities are sources of funds;
 (iv) Decreases in liabilities are uses of funds.

With these simple rules, one can prepare a funds flow analysis for any company from the published accounts.

It is also possible to explain the change in the cash position between the two Balance Sheets in terms of the flow of funds. Where this is done, in the four rules given above read 'cash' for 'funds'. For Currys' 1979 Balance Sheet the explanation for the increase in cash holding of £388,000 (from £428,000 to £816,000) is:

CASH MOVEMENT 1979

		£'000s
Opening Cash Balance		
Add		428
Decrease in ACT	86	
Increase in Creditors	2,664	
Increase in General Reserve	3,110	
Increase in Inflation Reserve	3,750	9,610
		10,038

Less

Increase in Fixed Assets	1,497	
Increase in Stock	4,768	
Increase in Credit Accounts	1,248	
Increase in Debtors	154	
Increase in payments in advance	90	
Increase in short-term deposits	375	
Decrease in taxation	966	
Decrease in dividend	124	9,222
Closing Cash Balance		£ 816

If the Funds Flow Statement covers several years it illustrates the available sources of funds. One can answer questions such as: Where is the company obtaining its finance? How much is from internally generated sources – retained profit and depreciation, the cash flow of the firm? How much is coming from increases in short-term liabilities – not paying creditors on time, or increasing overdraft facilities? How much from the raising of long-term loans or fresh issues of capital? And how is the amount available being used? How much is being put into fixed assets, or invested in increased stockholding or credit to customers? The Funds Flow Statement provides the key to understanding the financial movements of the company's management. It tells one where management is obtaining finance, and how it is being used.

Combined with analysis of the ratios described in Chapter 2 funds flow analysis gives the maximum information that can be extracted from a company's Annual Report. The Currys' Statement is set out in Fig. 5.1 from the 1979 Annual Report.

Following SSAP 10 all companies present such statements in their reports, and these are subject to audit. The form of presentation adopted in these Source and Application of Funds Statements differs from that used above to explain the mechanics of such statements. But Currys' Statement provides answers to the two basic questions, where the company generated its funds during the year 1979 and how they were used. Funds of £13.551m were provided from the operations of the company, and a further £1.185m from the sale of various fixed assets; from these sources £10.377m was used to finance the increase in working capital. All the figures in this Source and Application of Funds Statement can be found either in the Profit and Loss Account and Balance Sheet or in the notes which follow these in the company's Annual Report.

5.2 RATIOS AS PREDICTORS OF FUNDS FLOWS

The same ratios which are used to inform about past experience or the

86

Fig.5.1

Currys Limited

Statement of Source and Application of Group Funds
Year ended 24th January 1979

		1979 £'000		1978 £'000
Source of funds:				
Trading profit before taxation		10,885		9,218
Interest receivable less payable		960		529
Adjustment for items not involving the outlay of funds:				
Amortisation and depreciation		1,706		1,526
Funds generated from trading		13,551		11,273
Proceeds from sale of fixed assets		1,185		1,295
		14,736		12,568
Application of funds:				
Dividends paid	1,348		976	
Taxation paid	4,993		2,488	
Purchase of fixed assets	4,036		2,472	
		10,377		5,936
		4,359		6,632
Working capital movement:				
Increase in stocks		4,768		925
Increase in credit trading accounts, debtors and payments in advance		1,492		2,592
(Increase) in trade creditors		(2,664)		(2,113)
Movement in net liquid funds:				
Increase (decrease) in bank balances and cash	388		(47)	
Increase in short term deposits	375		5,275	
		763		5,228
		4,359		6,632

current situation can be used to explore the financial implications of management policies. For example, it is not unusual for a company to take a longer term decision without fully assessing its financial impact. The company below has a turnover of £1,200,000 per year, and depreciates its fixed assets on a straight-line basis of £50,000 per year.

BALANCE SHEET, 31 DECEMBER – I

Shareholders' Interest	400,000	Fixed Assets		200,000
Current Liabilities	200,000	Current Assets:		
		Stock	200,000	
		Debtors	100,000	
		Cash	100,000	400,000
	£600,000			£600,000

With a novel marketing campaign, the company believes it can double its turnover in the coming year and produce net profits of £100,000. This plan is enthusiastically and successfully carried out. The following year shows the Balance Sheet as:

BALANCE SHEET, 31 DECEMBER – II

Shareholders' Interest	500,000	Fixed Assets		150,000
Current Liabilities	400,000	Current Assets:		
		Stock	350,000	
		Debtors	400,000	
		Cash	–	750,000
	£900,000			£900,000

The company has indeed achieved its plan but, amid the euphoria, its accountant dismally points out the financial problems. The current ratio has moved from 2:1 to 1.9:1, and the 'acid test' remained constant at 1:1, but the company has no cash to carry on its operations. An emergency trip to the bank manager is called for.

The series of simple calculations outlined below could have shown this possibility to the company's management before the plan was put into operation, and enabled them to negotiate ahead of time with the bank. Money required at short notice can be expensive.

(a) Financing debtors and stock
The company was allowing approximately thirty days' credit to customers – one month's sales appear as debtors in the first year's Balance Sheet. Had management been asked what credit they would have to extend to double sales, they might have predicted sixty days. From this it would be possible to predict what the debtors figure would be in the next year's

Balance Sheet:

$$\frac{60}{365} = \text{one-sixth of predicted sales of £2,400,000}$$

$$= £400,000$$

Ignoring all else for the moment, management could have asked the questions: how is this £300,000 increase in debtors to be financed? Can the company afford it?

To answer that question, funds flow analysis can be used. What are the sources of funds going to be during the next year?

Profit	£100,000	
Depreciation	50,000	
	150,000	
Cash	100,000	£250,000

Even including the £100,000 cash balance, there will only be £250,000 available, and this is insufficient to meet the £300,000 extra debtors. The company must therefore either slow down on the payment of creditors, obtain overdraft facilities from the bank, or obtain longer term loans. At the beginning of the year, while management is still considering its plans, it would be possible to show that the likely increase in debtors would stretch the company's finances considerably.

If the likely change in stock is also considered, then the probable year-end financial picture becomes clearer. The company is turning its stock over approximately once every two months; the ratio of sales to stock in year 1 was six times per year. If the company's management had been asked at the beginning of the year what the likely impact on stock would be of the doubling of turnover, they might have felt that stockholding would not have to double with sales, and they could achieve a stock turnover of approximately seven times per year. Such a forecast stock turnover would have shown that at the year end there would be £343,000 stock — one-seventh of £2,400,000.

Thus, if the increase in stock of £143,000 is added to the increase in debtors of £300,000, it can be forecast that the company must find finance for an additional £443,000 in order to achieve its plan of doubling sales revenue. To do this would require running down the cash resources, and increasing the short-term borrowing from creditors, perhaps to the detriment of future relations.

Had this information been available to the company it could have planned either to moderate the increase in sales, or to borrow well in advance of any crisis.

(b) Creditors

The same calculations for debtors can be carried out for creditors. But here the level of creditors should be related to the purchases that are made. If, in the example given above, purchases of materials had accounted for £800,000 in the first year, and the whole £200,000 current liabilities represented these materials creditors, then the length of credit can be seen to be:

$$365 \div \frac{£800,000}{£200,000} = 91 \text{ days}$$

If the company were expecting to be able to maintain these generous relationships with the increased sales, then if ninety-one days' credit is taken on £1,600,000 of materials purchases the figure for current liabilities in the next year's Balance Sheet would be:

$$\frac{91}{365} = \frac{1}{4} \times £1,600,000$$

$$= £400,000$$

Using these simple ratios it is possible to draft a pro-forma Balance Sheet to help management assess the financial implications of their plans.

If the company thought it possible to increase further the credit taken from suppliers to 120 days, then it would show in the pro-forma Balance Sheet for the next year:

$$\frac{120}{365} = \frac{1}{3} \times £1,600,000$$

$$= £533,000$$

This additional £133,000 (£533,000 − £400,000 current liabilities) could be used to finance the increase in stock and debtors required under the plan for doubling turnover. The pro forma Balance Sheet for the end of the next year would then appear as follows:

PRO FORMA BALANCE SHEET, 31 DECEMBER — II

Shareholders' Interest	500,000	Fixed Assets		150,000
Current Liabilities	533,000	Current Assets:		
		Stock	343,000	
		Debtors	400,000	
		Cash	140,000	883,000
	£1,033,000			£1,033,000

A Funds Flow Statement would show the changes from the first Balance Sheet:

Sources		Uses	
Retained profit	100,000	Increase in stock	143,000
Depreciation	50,000	Increase in debtors	300,000
Increase in current liabilities	333,000	Increase in cash	40,000
	£483,000		£483,000

This kind of analysis, in which ratios are used to predict future figures rather than to interpret historic ones, is undertaken in most financially aware companies when assessing plans and investment programmes. In the light of historic experience, the figures produced are essential for assessing the impact of plans on the company's financial state.

5.3 THE OPERATING CYCLE

The operating cycle is the time taken from the initial input of funds into raw materials to the final receipt of funds from customers after the goods containing those materials have been sold. Measurement of the operating cycle requires the combination of a series of ratios to provide useful information.

THE OPERATING CYCLE

Days

$$\text{Raw materials turnover} = \frac{\text{Average raw materials stock}}{\text{Average daily materials purchases}} =$$

less

$$\text{Credit taken on materials} = \frac{\text{Average creditors}}{\text{Average daily materials purchases}} =$$

add

$$\text{Production time} = \frac{\text{Average work-in-progress}}{\text{Average daily cost of goods sold}} =$$

$$\text{Finished goods turnover} = \frac{\text{Average finished stock}}{\text{Average daily cost of goods sold}} =$$

$$\text{Credit allowed} = \frac{\text{Average debtors}}{\text{Average daily sales}} =$$

Time (in days) of operating cycle = _____

Each ratio in the operating cycle measures an aspect of the firm's work. The raw materials turnover tells how long the company's funds are employed in this area. The average stock is found by taking the opening and closing stocks and dividing by two; the average daily purchases by taking the total of purchases for the year and dividing by 365. From this is deducted the average length of credit taken by the firm to show the net time funds are employed in raw materials. The operating cycle then follows through into production and eventual finished stock with similar calculations. The final ratio is that of the credit period allowed by the firm to customers.

The shorter the operating cycle, the better the use of available funds. From the calculations for the cycle a company can quickly see the bottlenecks in its operations. Which point in the cycle is the slowest, and why? The ratios in the operating cycle do not answer any questions. They merely indicate that questions should be asked of the relevant areas of the firm's operations.

5.4 FINANCIAL PLANNING

The chairman of a small manufacturing company once said, 'We haven't time for plans; we just make a profit'. In smaller companies planning is often seen as a waste of effort, since by the time the plans are completed, many of the factors and assumptions will have changed, and in any case key personnel are too busy getting and running the business. Yet one often finds in such cases that the key managers have a good idea of where they are going and where they wish to be, and how to react if things go off course – even if the planning process is not done formally according to planning textbooks. Nevertheless it is usually helpful to get such ideas out in the open, and to explore the financial implications, to ask such simple questions as:

   (i) What is the company's business?
  (ii) What are the key factors that will affect this in the future?
 (iii) What are the company's strengths?
 (iv) What are the company's weaknesses?
  (v) What are the limiting factors on future growth?

The answers may not be simple, obvious or commonly agreed, and the discussion that should be stimulated will cover not only the internal factors which bear on the company's future, but also many external factors such as:

   (i) competitive activities;
  (ii) government changes in legislation, taxation, and other policies;

    (iii) changes in social tastes and behaviour;
    (iv) economic changes;
    (v) technological changes.

Management will be making assumptions about how these factors will change in the future, and what their impact will be on the company's growth potential. If each manager or director writes down the assumptions he is making, then at least everyone will have an idea of how others view the future. It is all too common to embark on a planning process without agreement as to the framework upon which the plan is built. Much of the planning process is a mechanical exercise done by the accountants, but this is in many ways the least important part. The difficult part is deciding how the company must be directed through the uncertainties of the future. This is the responsibility of management. Corporate planning is discussed in more detail in Chapter 11.

The accountant's function in this is to assist management to see clearly the financial implications of proposed policies and plans, and to choose between the alternative strategies.

A key factor that most boards will consider in planning for the future is profitability. No company can survive the long term without profitability. But perhaps profit is more of a means to an end than an end in itself for many modern businesses. The board must be concerned to ensure sufficient profit or growth for shareholders, to pay employees good wages, and to provide funds for the capital investment necessary to maintain the company's growth. Profit is an expression of the company's goal. How the profit should be used or distributed is a particular issue that depends on the goals of the company's shareholders, directors and other interested parties.

When management have produced their forecasts of sales, costs and profit, together with capital investment proposals, they must bring them all together in a Master Financial Forecast. This is best done along the lines of funds flow analysis. Where is the company going to generate the funds, and how are these funds to be used? This can be set out in the table as follows:

MASTER FINANCIAL FORECAST, YEAR 1–5

Major uses of funds	Year 1	2	3	4	5
Capital investments					
Repayments of loans	——	—	—	—	—
Major sources of funds					
Pre-tax profit					
Depreciation	——	—	—	—	—
Surplus/Deficit	══	=	=	=	=

Changes in working capital
   Increase/Decrease in stock
   Increase/Decrease in debtors
   Increase/Decrease in cash
   Increase/Decrease in creditors
   Increase/Decrease in taxation
   Increase/Decrease in dividend
   Increase/Decrease in overdraft

   Net change in working capital

Overall surplus/deficit of funds in year

This table provides management with the basis for assessing the funds requirements of the company over the next five years on the basis of the various forecasts and assumptions. If a deficit is shown, management can consider whether to raise funds with long-term loans or fresh capital issues, or to approach a bank for a short- or medium-term financing agreement.

The table can also be used to test the sensitivity of financial requirements to the various component items. For example, if there is a minor deficit in one year, could this be overcome by changing the debtor and stock position rather than by borrowing funds? It will also be possible to assess the impact of delaying capital investment programmes by one year on the finance requirements. Such factors can be looked at by management until the final result is agreed and becomes the Five-Year Financial Plan, the stated funds flow that management is to achieve over the next five years — a statement of intention, the plan.

Of course, completion of this plan does not guarantee that all will go as predicted. Indeed, the only thing certain is that the plan will not be met. Matters will change in a way the company could not predict. This argument is often used against formal planning exercises. But it is still beneficial for managers to have thought about their business in these terms, and have a plan against which to consider the changes as they occur. There is a basis for comparison and control, which would not be available if planning were ignored. Management is more likely to react reasonably to changing circumstances after planning than if none had been done. However, this does require an ability to recognise when cherished hopes are going awry. Then the financial impacts of changes can be quickly fed into the planning table and new decisions and policy made.

The long-term overall planning exercise has been outlined above. Part of this is the cash budgeting process, by which companies plan for, and monitor, their flow of cash over shorter time periods — normally twelve months.

94

5.5 CASH BUDGETING

Most companies must practise cash budgeting in some degree. If they use a
bank overdraft, the bank usually expects some form of cash budget, and
certainly expects the company's cash position to fluctuate within the
agreed overdraft limit, thus to this extent the company must manage its
cash flows. If the company does not use overdraft facilities it must manage
its cash flow so as not to overdraw its account.

A cash budget is a statement of the flow of cash expected over a given
time period. In simple terms a cash budget can be seen as:

	£
Opening cash balance	
Add Cash from sales	
Cash from other sources	———————
Total cash available	
Less Cash paid for materials	
Cash paid for wages	
Cash paid for expenses	
Other cash payments	———————
Closing cash balance	£ =========

The expected cash inflows during the period are added to the opening
cash balance to provide the total amount of cash available during that
period. From this amount the expected cash payments are deducted to
produce the closing cash balance, which is carried forward as the next
period's opening cash balance.

For a twelve-month cash budget information will be needed on sales for
that period, the credit to be allowed customers (this will affect the timing
of the cash receipts), and the amount and timing of all cash payments
(whether for direct costs such as wages and materials, or indirect costs
such as rent, rates and insurance). The cash budget reflects the cash
consequences of the company's operations. Plans are translated into the
impact on the cash balance of the company just as with the financial
forecast and plan, but in more detail.

With such a cash budget, management can see which months are likely
to be critical as far as cash is concerned, whether the timing of expenditure
is appropriate, and at the beginning of the year plan their cash position for
the coming twelve months, so that overdraft facilities can be negotiated
well in advance, and the bank shown how and when they will be repaid.
The following example illustrates the production of a cash budget over a
four-month period. The following information is collected:

(a) Sales

Sales are normally 50 per cent for cash, 25 per cent on credit with payment received in the month following the sale, and 25 per cent on credit to one large customer who pays two months after the date of sale. There are no discounts. Sales are expected to be:

December (actual)		£40,000
January		60,000
February	(budget)	80,000
March		60,000
April		40,000

This information can be set out as in Table 1:

TABLE 1
SALES AND CASH INFLOW

	December	January	February	March	April
Sales in month	£40,000	60,000	80,000	60,000	40,000
Cash received in month:					
December	20,000	10,000	10,000		
January		30,000	15,000	15,000	
February			40,000	20,000	20,000
March				30,000	15,000
April					20,000
	£20,000	40,000	65,000	65,000	55,000

(b) Other costs and expenses

From the budgets and forecasts the following information was collected on the costs and expenses associated with sales:

TABLE 2
COSTS AND EXPENSES
(Month of occurrence)

	December	January	February	March	April	4-month total
Materials	£15,000	35,000	30,000	20,000	20,000	(105,000)
Wages	10,000	10,000	20,000	12,000	10,000	(52,000)
Other expenses	10,000	10,000	20,000	10,000	10,000	(50,000)
Capital expenditure			15,000			(15,000)

(i) Materials are paid for in the month following delivery with no discounts allowed.

(ii) Wages are paid one-half in the month incurred and one-half in the following month.

(iii) Other expenses are paid in the month following.

(iv) The capital expenditure is for a new machine to be installed and paid for in February.

(c) Other information

The company maintains a base stock of raw materials and finished goods of £5,000. This is to be continued into the coming year, and the materials purchases are those necessary to service the sales budget, and maintain the minimum £5,000 stock level.

The company has fixed assets with a written-down value of £100,000 on 31 December. These are depreciated at £30,000 per annum.

The shareholders' interest in the company on 31 December was £97,000.

On 31 December the company had a cash balance of £2,000.

From this information it is possible to draft the Balance Sheet as at 31 December, the Cash Budget for the coming four months, and a set of accounts covering the same period.

BALANCE SHEET, 31 DECEMBER

	£		£
Shareholders' Interest	97,000	Fixed Assets	100,000
Current Liabilities:		Current Assets:	
Creditors:		Stock 5,000	
Materials	15,000	Debtors 20,000	
Wages	5,000	Cash 2,000	27,000
Other	10,000 30,000		
	£127,000		£127,000

CASH BUDGET, JANUARY–APRIL

	January	February	March	April	Amount still due
Opening cash balance	2,000	7,000	(3,000)	(4,000)	
Cash from sales	40,000	65,000	65,000	55,000	(35,000)
Total cash available	42,000	72,000	62,000	51,000	

(continued)

	January	February	March	April	Amount still due
Cash payments:					
Materials	15,000	35,000	30,000	20,000	(20,000)
Wages	10,000	15,000	16,000	11,000	(5,000)
Other	10,000	10,000	20,000	10,000	(10,000)
Capital		15,000			
Total cash out in month	35,000	75,000	66,000	41,000	
Closing cash balance	7,000	(3,000)	(4,000)	10,000	

PROFIT AND LOSS ACCOUNT FOR THE FOUR MONTHS ENDED 30 APRIL

Materials used		105,000	Sales	240,000
Wages		52,000		
Other expenses		50,000		
Depreciation:				
Old plant	10,000			
New plant	1,000	11,000		
Profit		22,000		
		£240,000		£240,000

BALANCE SHEET AS AT 30 APRIL

Shareholders' Interest:			Fixed Assets:		
December balance	97,000		December balance	100,000	
Profit and Loss Account	22,000	119,000	February addition	15,000	
				115,000	
			Depreciation	11,000	104,000
Current Liabilities:			Current Assets:		
Creditors:			Stock	5,000	
Materials (April)	20,000		Debtors (¼ March		
Wages (½ April)	5,000		+ ½ April)	35,000	
Other (April)	10,000	35,000	Cash	10,000	50,000
		£154,000			£154,000

Once the Cash Budget and pro-forma accounts for the four months have been completed, management can consider their implications. The Profit and Loss Account shows a good profit, and the April working capital situation is much sounder. But the Cash Budget shows that during February and March the company will have to borrow around £4,000 if the budgeted level of activity is to be maintained. This shortage of cash is due mainly to the cash purchase of the new machine in February. Management can decide whether to obtain an overdraft for the two months, or to delay the purchase of the machine until April, when borrowing will not be necessary if all goes according to budget.

This simplified example highlights the mechanics and benefits of cash budgeting. If a company produces a cash budget for twelve months it has a statement in cash terms of the impact of its budgeted activity. Planned sales, costs, expenses and capital outlays are put together to show the cash movements, and to highlight danger points. With this foreknowledge, management can in advance approach the bank, raise long-term capital, or change the pattern and timing of income and expenditure.

With volatile or unpredictable sales, it may not be feasible to produce a detailed annual cash budget, but it should be possible for every company to draft a shorter period budget, such as three or four months ahead. And in any case a worst and best case forecast should show the sensitivity of the cash balance to changes in sales and expenses.

Planning the cash movements and deciding how much cash to hold can be a key task. Cash by itself is a wasteful asset. It does not earn profit — except when placed on deposit, and then it will earn less than if employed in the business. The cash budget will show whether the company is maintaining sufficient cash resources throughout the budget or, if too much cash is expected to be generated, plans can be made for its investment either in the firm or outside.

Cash turnover is the measure of the circulation of cash, the velocity of cash movement. The ratio is similar for stock turnover, but with the average cash balance as the denominator:

$$\text{Cash turnover} = \frac{\text{Sales}}{\text{Average cash balance}}$$

Different industries will exhibit different cash turnovers, and firms within the same industry will often have quite different ratios. For example Pilkington in 1979 had a cash turnover of 9 and cash represented some 21 per cent of Current Assets. The 1979 ratios for two other firms were:

	Tesco	Currys
Cash turnover	54	308
Cash as a % of current assets	17	1

This sort of comparison can be misleading, however, for if short-term deposits are included in the liquid resources of Currys, the ratios become 13 and 25 per cent respectively for the cash turnover and percentage of current assets. The cash budgeting exercise will probably raise the question of what credit policy should be adopted, and how to monitor the level of debtors. The general credit period allowed will partly depend on trade, custom and other marketing considerations, partly on the financial state of the company. A helpful aid to monitoring the credit period is to complete each month an age analysis of debtors, showing the age of the debts due to the company.

DEBTOR AGE ANALYSIS REPORT

Total sales debtors at end of month . . . . £

Age of debt	Amount £	% of total
Less than 1 month	. . .	. . .
1 to 2 months	. . .	. . .
2 to 3 months	. . .	. . .
Over 3 months	. . .	. . .
	. . .	. . .

With long overdue debtors, this analysis will raise the question why there has been a delay in collecting cash, and what steps are being taken to rectify the situation. A similar exercise could be conducted in relation to creditors.

5.6 PREDICTING BANKRUPTCY

The search for the key to unlock the Balance Sheet and predict financial disaster has been for years to accountants as the touchstone was to the alchemists. Somewhere in the Balance Sheet there must be indicators of impending bankruptcy. It has always been possible to employ funds flow analysis to this end, using historical data and assumptions as to the future to provide some clues. If a company's funds flow has been declining and is expected to continue to do so, then a simple extrapolation using ordinary Balance Sheet ratios can show when it is likely to become critical, calling for outside finance or complete reorganisation.

In the late 1960s Professor E. I. Altman[1] investigated whether Balance Sheet ratios could provide good predictions of bankruptcy. His and subsequent findings appear to indicate some basis for a belief that this is possible. Using 'multiple discriminant analysis' – a variation on multiple regression analysis – he produced the following function, on the basis of a large set of US Corporate Bankruptcies:

$$Z = 0.012a + 0.014b + 0.033c + 0.006d + 0.999e$$

where a = working capital/total assets
b = retained earnings/total assets
c = earnings before interest and tax/total assets
d = market value of equity/book value of total debt
e = sales/total assets.

The first four ratios are all expressed as percentages, and the final one is the asset turnover ratio. In ratio b retained earnings means the total amount of retained profit appearing in the Balance Sheet, and ratio c measures the pre-tax-and-interest profit for the year as a percentage of total assets. Ratio d uses the 'capitalisation' of the company (the number of shares issued, multiplied by their market value) divided by the liabilities of the company excluding shareholders' interest.

If the five ratios are calculated for a company, and weighted according to the formula, the Z factor can be used as an indicator of the future financial health of the company. This shows how ratios can be used in conjunction with statistical techniques to provide useful information. If the Z factor is over 3, the firm is unlikely to go bankrupt in the coming year; if under 2, the firm is likely to have severe financial problems.

6 Sources of Business Finance

Every growing company is faced with the problem of financing its growth. Few companies can finance business development entirely from their own operations. Funds requirements will be greater than funds generation at certain points of time. So how, and where, should the additional finance be raised?

One experienced financier has suggested that 'if the money is available, and looks cheap, borrow it even if you don't need it immediately'. With the inflation of the past few years this advice would have stood many companies in good stead. It is always better to borrow, or arrange to borrow, funds well in advance of their need. Failure to look for finance before it is needed is a sign of bad management. Chapter 5 outlined the method of longer range financial planning and of shorter-term cash budgeting which provides management with ample warning of future funds requirements. This chapter outlines the means of meeting these financial requirements.

These can be broadly classified into two types – short-term requirements, and the need for longer, perhaps permanent, finance. We consider first the various sources and types of short-term finance.

6.1 SHORT- AND MEDIUM-TERM FINANCE

(a) Bank borrowing
In the Balance Sheet a company's finance is divided into only two categories – short-term (less than one year) and long-term (more than one year). But in the financial markets this 'long-term' is normally divided into medium- and long-term, with the actual terms depending on company and industry investment lead-times and on banking convention. As a rule of thumb, one to five years is medium-term, beyond that, long-term.

The best known, and most frequently used, source of short-term finance

101

in the UK is the bank overdraft. Every company has at least one bank account with one of the UK clearing banks.

These banks are in the business of lending money, and have developed a range of services to assist companies of all sizes with their financial needs. In recent years banks have moved into the medium- to long-term loan area, and it is now possible to obtain ten-year loans from most UK banks, but the main emphasis is still on short-term finance.

Theoretically the overdraft is repayable to the bank on demand − this is why it is always shown as a current liability in the Balance Sheet − but in practice this is rarely demanded, or feasible, without winding the company up. However, during the 'squeeze' in the early 1970s pressure was applied to many firms by their banks to repay or reduce their overdrafts.

The advantage of overdraft financing is its flexibility. Within an agreed overdraft limit a company can manage its affairs as it sees fit. If the total offered is not used, then no interest is paid on the unused part. If the overdraft is paid off earlier than expected, no interest is due on the unused, but available, balance.

In approaching a bank for an overdraft a company should prepare a detailed cash flow forecast − a cash budget that will provide the banker with answers to the main questions he will raise:

   (i) How is the money to be used?
  (ii) How much money is required?
 (iii) When is the money required?
 (iv) When will the money be repaid?

This cash budget is based on a forecast of future business. It should be supported by the latest accounts of the company. The bank will also check its own records, a history of the company's previous dealings with the bank and details of the individuals concerned.

The banker is making a judgement on the company, while the company may in turn be shopping for the best terms. Ability to present and analyse past performance, present and future prospects, and their financial implications, is itself a way of demonstrating competent management.

With this information the banker, whether branch manager or specialist loan officer, can assess the viability of the proposal, based on his own criteria and the relative availability of finance. First he will decide how much he can offer, with or without security, and at what rate of interest. The rate of interest depends mainly on the degree of risk that the banker associates with the proposal. It will be quoted at a percentage above the ruling bank rate.

From the bank's view the ideal overdraft is self-liquidating − that is, the loan will be repaid out of the continued operations of the business. For example, if the bank allows an overdraft for a few months while a company builds up stocks of finished goods, it will expect to see the overdraft repaid later in the year from the proceeds of the sale of these goods. Thus the overdraft is ideally suited to accommodating short-term fluctuations in business, such as seasonal sales, where manufacture and stocks have to be financed in advance. Yet the accounts of many large public companies show that the overdraft forms an almost permanent part of their capital structure, sometimes beyond their need for short-term finance.

The flexibility of the overdraft facility, the ability to draw and repay, within an agreed limit, makes it the easiest and probably the cheapest form of finance available. Consequently companies tend to make full use of it.

(b) Trade credit

Delaying payment of creditors is a form of short-term finance often used by individuals as well as companies. But the longer term consequences must be considered. The goodwill of the supplier may be pushed to the limit, and produce a reluctance to supply more materials without immediate payment of previous bills. The supplier may also prove reluctant to provide special service in a crisis, and the reputation for being a bad payer can also hamper relations with other suppliers or a local community.

Most suppliers provide some form of credit to established companies. But in order to expedite payment they often offer discounts for cash, or for prompt payment. These apparently small discounts nearly always offer a financial advantage. For example, if a supplier delivers goods valued at £1,000, offering a discount of 2 per cent if the bill is paid within thirty days, the company should whenever possible take the discount. The reason is that the real rate of discount is much higher than 2 per cent.

$$\frac{£20}{£980} \times \frac{365 \text{ days}}{30 \text{ days}} = 25\% \text{ per annum}$$

As a simple rule of thumb, the annual equivalent of 1 per cent per month is approximately 13 per cent per annum.

This annual rate of interest represents the real advantage the company would be missing if it did not take the available discount. Other things being equal, so long as the real cost of a bank overdraft (interest plus commission) is below 25 per cent per annum, it will pay to take trade discounts at 25 per cent using overdraft finance. Conversely, these calculations suggest that companies should be careful about the discounts they offer customers for prompt payment.

Discounts are part of the competitive package (including price, product quality, delivery, service, range of goods etc.) offered by firms in industrial markets. The criteria for choice of a supplier should include assessment of its credit and payment terms.

(c) Factoring and Invoice Discounting

The factoring of debts is the selling of a company's debts to another firm on a regular basis. The 'factor' then owns these debts, and maintains the necessary book-keeping records and credit control mechanisms, and collects these debts on its own behalf. Invoice discounting is the selling of the company's debts at a particular point in time so as to release funds tied up in them. Both these methods involve the transfer of legal title to the debts to a third party.

Factoring and invoice discounting release up to 90 per cent of the value of invoices, which can be a very useful source of immediate funds. But the costs associated with this are 1–3 per cent of sales value, much higher than bank overdraft rates. In addition to the financial benefit of generating cash sales, factoring can relieve a company of the administrative costs of book-keeping, invoicing and credit control. Furthermore, if the market is not very price-sensitive, the cost of factoring can be recovered by a relatively small price rise.

(d) Bills of Exchange

A bill of exchange is a kind of postdated cheque. It allows a company time to pay the bill together with interest. The company owing the money 'accepts' the bill, by writing 'accepted' on it, and when it comes due for payment (when it matures) the amount plus interest is paid to whoever holds it. The company which has the right to payment on the bill can sell, or 'negotiate', the bill with a bank or any other person or institution. In so doing it will sell at lower than face value, thus discounting the bill.

Bills of exchange are acceptable for relatively large amounts from established institutions, and therefore they can only really be used by larger companies as a source of funds approximating in cost to that of bank overdraft facilities. But there is no reason why smaller companies dealing with large ones should not obtain bills of exchange which they can then discount for cash.

(e) Hire-purchase

Hire-purchase can be as attractive to a company as to an individual. Under this system the total cost of an item is not paid all at once, but spread over a period, with weekly or monthly instalments. This spreads the cost of the asset over time, approximating the timing of payments to that of incoming benefits.

Not only is the capital cost of the asset paid, but also an interest charge. The real cost of hire-purchase will vary from firm to firm, but is often more than double the cost of overdraft facilities. Hire-purchase is therefore expensive, but a company using hire-purchase to obtain an asset for its business may be able to claim tax allowance on it in just the same manner as if the asset were wholly owned. Typically, under hire-purchase, title to the asset does not pass to the purchaser until all payments have been completed.

(f) Leasing

Almost any plant, machinery, buildings or equipment that a company may need can be leased. The decision whether to buy or lease assets will depend on its overall planning and projected cash flow. If leased, the asset can be used in just the same manner as if it were purchased, but a regular cash outflow will be experienced as the rental is paid.

'Sale and lease-back' is a common form of freeing cash from fixed assets. Under this method a company which owns an asset can sell it to an insurance company or finance institution or other concern, and lease it back at an agreed rate. This can free large amounts of cash for the company without in any way altering the use of physical assets.

(g) Merchant Banks and Venture Capital

Merchant banks and other financial institutions are always looking for companies with growth potential, in need of money to maintain or increase profitable growth. This is particularly true where the company can use such finance to grow to a size that makes an offer of shares to the public possible. This is the provision of venture capital. The firm providing it puts money in a company in return for shares or other loan agreements that can be converted in the future into shares. The intention is to make a good return once the shares are offered to the public.

This form of finance enables a company to obtain £50,000 to £500,000 on very competitive terms, together with much helpful financial advice from the professionals employed by the lending company. However, a company using this source of funds must expect to release some portion of its equity in return for the loan, and possibly accept an outsider on the Board and submit itself to scrutiny. This dilution of ownership and control may sometimes be unacceptable to directors who have built a company up from scratch.

6.2 LONG-TERM FINANCE

A company which already has a stock exchange quotation can offer additional shares to the public to raise further funds to continue the business. There are various ways of doing this.

(i) *Public issue.* The company offers the public its shares, using a prospectus which contains all the information considered necessary both by government legislation and by stock exchange requirements. The shares are offered at a fixed price and the public apply for the number they require.

(ii) *Offer for sale.* With a prospectus containing details of the company's history and potential the shares are offered to the public, not by the company, but by one of the financial institutions. The financial institution purchases all the shares from the company at an agreed price, and then offers them to the public at a higher price. The margin made on the issue replaces the fee which would have been charged for assistance with a public issue. Under this method the company is guaranteed a fixed sum of capital, while the financial institution bears the risk in case the issue is not fully taken up by the public.

(iii) *Placing.* With this method the shares that are to be offered, or the majority of those shares, are sold privately by the financial institution to its clients. This method is only suitable for smaller share issues.

(iv) *Sale by tender.* This is similar to an offer for sale except that there is a minimum price set on the shares, and offers are invited. The person wishing to purchase shares states the price he is willing to pay and the number he requires. The shares are then allocated on the basis of the best bids that will take up all the shares offered.

(v) *Rights issue.* Existing shareholders are offered the right to purchase new shares in proportion to their holding of the company's existing issued shares. The price at which the shares are offered is below the current market price of that class of shares in the company.

There are other types of share issue, but these are not really concerned with raising funds for operations:

(vi) *Scrip issue.* Where the company has a high proportion of its shareholders' interest made up of reserves — either retained profit or capital reserves — the dividend that is paid to shareholders can often appear excessive when related to the number of shares issued rather than their total investment in the company, the shareholders' interest. To change this the company can issue shares to existing shareholders that convert the reserves into shares. This is often termed a scrip issue. It is the capitalisation of reserves. It makes no real difference to the shareholders except that they will have more shares, and the company show less reserves.

(vii) *Share split.* Sometimes a company's shares reach such a high price that it is difficult to deal in small units of them. If a £1 share has a market value of £50, a company may decide to split the £1 share into 50 2p shares. This raises no additional cash for the company, and does not affect the shareholder except that he now has 50 shares each worth £1 instead of one worth £50, and can sell some of his holding more easily than before. It is also possible to reverse this procedure and consolidate a number of small-value shares into one of larger value.

The cost of issuing shares can be considerable and should be considered as part of the cost of raising capital in this way. There are legal costs, accountant's fees for providing the various special reports necessary, and also advertising and printing costs as well as any underwriting commission.

Share issues can be underwritten by an issuing house, that is, a financial institution will guarantee that any shares that are not taken up in the issue will be purchased. For this guarantee they will charge an underwriting commission.

The mechanics of issuing shares are relatively simple. The critical question is what sort of shares to issue and, most important, at what price. If the company offers shares at too low a price, then it will have lost an opportunity to raise funds, and the benefit accrues to the purchasers as the market price rises. If the price is too high it may not raise as much as expected. If a company and its advisers have got the issue price right, dealings in the shares on the stock exchange immediately after the issue tend to be at 5–10 per cent above the issue price.

6.3 TYPES OF CAPITAL

We have discussed above the various means by which shares can be issued to increase the funds available. But there is a variety of shares and debentures which can be issued.

(a) Equity capital

The equity capital of a company is made up of its ordinary shares. These are the shares that have a right to participate in the profits of the company by way of dividends that are decided by the company's directors. They have no right to a fixed return, and the dividend will depend on the profits available for distribution after the directors have made all appropriations they see fit.

The ordinary shareholders will only receive payment of a dividend after all other shareholders have been satisfied by payment of their due dividend. There may be several classes of ordinary shares:

   (i) Preferred Ordinary
  (ii) Deferred Ordinary
 (iii) Founders' shares
  (iv) A Ordinary
   (v) B Ordinary

These types of shares will have different voting rights.

When funds are raised by issue of ordinary shares the only certain costs will be those of the actual issue. There is no requirement to maintain a fixed rate of dividend as with other forms of capital. If a company does not pay a dividend, retaining the profit for further growth, the market value of the ordinary shares can be expected to rise to compensate for the lack of dividend, and to reflect these future growth expectations.

The Balance Sheet of the company will show what is the authorised number and nominal value of ordinary shares that may be issued as well as the actual issued shares on that date. This value for the ordinary shares is the 'par value'. Thus, a company that has ordinary shares with a nominal value of £1 each has ordinary shares of £1 par value.

(b) Fixed capital

Preference shares have declined in attractiveness over the last decade. The reason for this decline in popularity is that preference shares receive a fixed rate of dividend, and under conditions of inflation this is not an attractive proposition. Preference shareholders are paid their dividend before the ordinary shareholder, and in the case of a liquidation they have prior claim to repayment before all other shareholders. There are various forms of preference share:

   (i) *Cumulative Preference.* These shares have the right to have any dividend not paid in one year carried over and added to the dividend due in the following year.
  (ii) *Participating Preference.* These have the right to share in profits not only with their own fixed dividend, but also after the ordinary shareholders have received a specified level of dividend.
 (iii) *Redeemable Preference.* These can be repurchased by the company. Only certain funds can be used for this purpose — profits otherwise available for dividends or funds from a new issue of shares made specifically for this purpose. When redemption is

made out of profits, an amount equal to the nominal value of the shares must be placed in a Capital Redemption Reserve Fund, and this fund can be used to make a scrip issue (Section 58, 1948 Companies Act).

(iv) *Convertible Preference.* These can be converted into ordinary shares at some future date, and at a specified price.

As preference shares have declined, the use of debentures has increased. These are more flexible and cheaper than preference shares. Interest on a debenture is allowable against the company's tax, while the dividend on a preference share is not.

(i) *Floating Debenture.* This is a loan which is secured by a floating charge on the company's assets.

(ii) *Fixed Debenture.* This is a loan which is secured on some particular asset, or assets, of the company — usually land and buildings. This means that the company cannot dispose of the asset at will; it must either pay off the debenture or obtain permission from the debenture holder.

(iii) *Convertible Debenture.* This is a debenture which has the right to be converted into ordinary shares at some future date and at an agreed price. This is a very popular method of providing venture capital to smaller firms. The institution providing the finance can obtain a reasonable rate of interest on the loan and also, by participating in the equity, share in the benefits of its growth.

6.4 CAPITAL GEARING

The term 'capital gearing' or 'leverage', is used to describe the relationship between the fixed-interest capital and the equity capital of a company. A 'highly geared' company is one which has a high proportion of fixed-interest capital compared with equity capital: a low-geared company has little fixed capital compared with ordinary shares, including reserves that form the shareholders' interest.

As with most of the terms so far discussed in this book, there are many alternative definitions. Capital gearing can also mean:

$$\text{Gearing} = \frac{\text{Ordinary share capital}}{\text{Preference share capital}}$$

$$\text{or} \quad = \frac{\text{Long-term finance and loans}}{\text{Total capital employed}}$$

$$\text{or} \quad = \frac{\text{Long-term debt}}{\text{Equity capital} + \text{long-term debt}}$$

To illustrate the importance of capital gearing, consider the three firms below:

	A	B	C
Ordinary share capital	3	2	0.5
Reserves	1	1	0.5
Fixed-interest capital	1	2	4.0
	£5	£5	£5

Using the most common measure of gearing – comparing the fixed-interest capital with shareholders' interest (not just the ordinary share capital) – the figures for these three firms are:

	A	B	C
Gearing ratio	0.25	0.67	4.0
Gearing	Low	Medium	High

If fixed-interest capital is raised, and can be used to earn a return in excess of the interest charge, then this goes to the ordinary shareholders of the company. This is the rationale for raising the gearing in a company's financial structure.

Thus, if companies A, B and C earn profits of £1 in the year, and the fixed-interest capital is at 10 per cent, then:

	A	B	C
Profit	1.0	1.0	1.0
Interest at 10%	0.1	0.2	0.4
Available for ordinary shares	£0.9	£0.8	£0.6

Thus, with the same profit, but different gearing, these firms produce varying profits for the ordinary shareholders of the company. This can be expressed as earnings per share:

	A	B	C
Number of ordinary shares	3	2	0.5
Profit	£0.9	£0.8	£0.6
Earnings per share	£0.3	£0.4	£1.2

The higher the gearing, the better the earnings per share for the ordinary shareholders. But with high gearing there is the risk of one year of low profits making it impossible to pay out all the required interest, and so management has to strike an acceptable balance. In the case of companies *A, B* and *C* if profit were to drop to £0.3, the earnings per share would become £0.07, £0.05 and −£0.2 respectively. With the high gearing in company *C* there would be a negative return to the ordinary shareholders because the profit would not cover the interest requirements of the year.

One way of expressing this is to compare the fixed-interest charge with the total profit earned before deducting that interest charge. For the three companies this is:

		A	*B*	*C*
$\dfrac{\text{Profit before interest}}{\text{Fixed-interest charge}}$	=	£1.0 / £0.1	£1.0 / £0.2	£1.0 / £0.4
Times interest covered =		10	5	2.5

A company which is making use of gearing must leave itself scope for the fluctuations in profit. Typically an interest cover of at least three or four times should be allowed, but the actual figure depends on the probability of a certain annual level of profits. If a company decides that a cover of five times is best for its needs, then this figure can be used to discover the maximum level of fixed interest the company can pay, and thereby the maximum amount of fixed-interest capital that the company should raise.

Another use of gearing levels is the amount of the company's finance that is being raised from current liabilities. This can be measured by the ratio:

$$\frac{\text{Current liabilities}}{\text{Shareholders' interest}} \quad \text{or} \quad \frac{\text{Current liabilities}}{\text{Net worth + Long-term finance}}$$

A company with a high ratio here probably has very little cushion against short-term fluctuations. If the maximum amount of credit is already being taken, with creditors stretched to the limit, then no more funds can be obtained from current liabilities if the need for short-term finance should arise.

6.5 CONCLUSION

This chapter has discussed the kinds of finance available to companies, but has not considered ways of choosing the best gearing or financing mix, or optimal strategies over time. Modern financial theory is mainly concerned with such optimising under conditions of risk, ignorance and uncertainty, and can be consulted in books on managerial finance which draw on this tradition.[1] For practical purposes, the devising of an optimal strategy is constrained by the quality of forecasts and other operating information available as inputs to decisions, and by limitations on available management time and ability. Nevertheless, managers should continually monitor the cost of finance and the company's financial mix under changing conditions, and as project plans are implemented.

It should also be remembered that the impact of inflation should be included in any assessment of future costs and returns. The time-value of money is discussed in Chapter 8.

7 The Stock Exchange

In Chapter 6 the various methods of raising finance were considered, together with alternative forms of short-, medium- and long-term capital. This chapter outlines the way in which institutions and individuals who influence or constitute the financial markets assess a company's performance. Accordingly, the more commonly used ratios are discussed in relation to the nature of the share market.

7.1 FINANCIAL INFORMATION REQUIRED

In assessing a company's current financial health, and historic performance record, the ratios discussed in Chapters 3 and 5 are of obvious importance, for they provide an indication of past success, and some early warning of future problems. But there are in addition a number of key ratios used by analysts, both amateur and professional, of company stocks. These are the ratios which appear, for instance, in the share information tables of *The Financial Times*, and other national newspapers and journals.

These ratios are made up from three pieces of information available in a company's Annual Report, and one external piece of information. The Accounts provide:

(i) the number of shares outstanding;
(ii) the net income for the year;
(iii) the dividend declared by the directors.

In addition, the market price of the stock is required — the price at which the shares of the company are changing hands on the stock market.

These basic building blocks in financial ratio analysis require some comment. For all can be defined in different ways, and it is easy to be misled if the information derived from different bases is applied as a performance yardstick.

First, the number of shares outstanding is the number of shares actually issued. This is not necessarily the same as the number of shares the company is authorised to issue. In the Balance Sheet this will be made clear under the section dealing with the net worth of the company. But the number of shares issued may be increased or decreased in the period following the publication of the Annual Report. A company may retire some of its own stock, or there may be a stock split or scrip issue, or stock options or conversions may be exercised.

Under a stock option scheme, the employees of a company may be given the option to purchase shares in the future at a predetermined price. If the company is successful, the share price will rise above the option price, providing the employees with a net capital gain when the options are exercised. The number of shares issued under such a scheme is normally small in relation to the total stock issued.

A similar scheme may involve 'convertible paper' such as preference shares or debentures. This resembles the stock option, in that it allows for purchase into common stock (ordinary shares) at a future date, but these issues may be made to the public as well as those institutions mentioned in the previous chapter. In return for putting up capital, the investor receives a debenture (which contains an obligation on behalf of the company to pay a fixed rate of interest) or preferred shares (which contain the requirement for a fixed rate of interest before, or in preference to, the common stockholders). When calculating the number of shares issued the investment analyst must check such changes in the balance between the various forms of finance following the exercising of convertible rights.

The second piece of information from the Annual Report is the net income or profit for the year. This was defined in some detail in Chapters 2 and 3. 'Net income' should be taken as net not only of debenture interest, which will have been deducted before corporation tax, but also of preferred stock dividends, which are payable after deduction of tax. For in analysing common stock prices, one is concerned only with the income attributable to, or earned by, that common stock.

Likewise, if comparisons are made between several years' performance or between companies, care must be taken to ensure that such comparison is based on common factors: like must be compared with like. The net income for a period may be affected by unusual or non-recurring items. Such items may result from an unusually large bad debt as a major customer is liquidated, or a capital gain on the sale of an asset.

The third piece of information is the dividend that the directors have declared for the year. Most large companies declare interim dividends, sometimes quarterly, sometimes half-yearly. These are aggregated to provide the total annual dividend.

Finally, there is the market price – the price at which shares are traded on the stock exchange. Most share prices, for reasons discussed later, undergo considerable fluctuations during any year. It is these fluctuations that make it necessary to publish share prices daily for the general public, and to monitor them continually on the stock exchange. Most share tables show the current year's lowest and highest price for any particular share. This provides the range, but not the trend.

7.2 BASIC STOCK EXCHANGE RATIOS

To illustrate the various stock exchange ratios used to assess company performance, we use a fictional company, Hedgebet Ltd, as an example. Hedgebet has 50,000 shares authorised, and has issued 40,000. The net of tax income for the current year is £80,000, and a dividend of £1 has been declared on the 40,000 ordinary shares issued. Thus £40,000 of the net of tax income is paid to the shareholders, and £40,000 retained in the company. The current market price of the shares is £16 each.

The earnings per share ratio shows what income was available for payment of the ordinary share dividend, and is found by dividing the net income by the total number of shares issued. For Hedgebet Ltd, this is:

$$\frac{\text{Net income}}{\text{Number of shares issued}} = \frac{£80,000}{40,000} = £2 \text{ per share}$$

(a) Price-earnings ratio

The earnings per share (EPS) figure is used in the calculation of the price-earnings ratio. This ratio has been used for many years in America, and over the last twenty years has become widely used in the UK as a key financial ratio both for company assessment and financial planning. It is calculated by taking the market price of the share, and dividing this by the earnings per share. For Hedgebet Ltd, this is:

$$\frac{\text{Market price of share}}{\text{Earnings per share}} = \frac{£16}{£2} = 8$$

The price-earnings ratio (P/E) is a very important one. It enables comparison to be made between all companies, between companies within an industry group, and between industries. In simple terms, the lower the P/E the lower the market's valuation of the share's future performance.

(b) Earnings cover

It is useful to know the number of times that the dividend is covered by net income. This is referred to as the 'times covered' or 'earnings cover' ratio. The ratio is calculated by dividing the net income by the amount of the dividend distribution. For Hedgebet Ltd, this is:

$$\frac{\text{Available income}}{\text{Dividend}} = \frac{£80,000}{£40,000} = 2 \text{ times covered}$$

Most companies retain at least some of their income in reserves, for reinvestment in the business.

(c) Earnings yield

It is important to assess the annual income accruing from an investment, and for this the percentage yield is calculated. This is done by taking the inverse of the P/E ratio which gives the 'capitalisation rate' or 'earnings yield'. This is the rate at which the market is capitalising the value of current earnings. In the example of the Hedgebet company:

$$\frac{\text{Earnings per share}}{\text{Market price of share}} \text{ or } \frac{1}{\text{P/E ratio}} = \frac{1}{8} = 12.5\%$$

This ratio enables a comparison to be made between shares and other interest-bearing investments. For the 12.5 per cent can be regarded as a form of interest earned by the stock. Note that it is not necessarily the historic interest rate (which would be the return based on the price at which an individual had purchased the stock), and also that it differs from interest-bearing investments in that on common stock all income is not usually distributed in dividends by the company.

The price-earnings ratio and the capitalisation rate, being ratios, are relative measures. If Hedgebet's earnings increase in the following year and the market price of the shares increases commensurately to take account of this, the P/E ratio and the capitalisation rate can remain the same, even though shareholders who have retained their shares since the previous year will have benefited from the increase in share price (in that the value of their holding will have increased) and from dividends (assuming that the company maintains its dividend policy).

For instance, if net income rises to £120,000, with the same number of shares outstanding, the earnings per share will be £3. If the market price rises proportionately the price will become £25, but the price-earnings ratio will remain the same as in the previous year, at 8 (£24/£3). The capitalisation rate will also remain constant at 12.5 per cent.

This underlines a key point about share information tables. They are always expressed in terms of current prices, for current buyers and sellers, while the earnings figure is the most recently declared. With the Hedgebet company one will now have to invest £24 to earn (assuming that earnings are the same next year) £3. In the previous year an investment of £16 apparently was providing income of £2. But in effect the investor buying a share at £16 last year has earned £1.50 dividend on the investment, and seen its value increase on the stock market by £8. The point that should be noted is that the real return on investment in shares consists of two components, the increase (or decrease) in the share's price, and the dividend payout. In the case of Hedgebet it could be said that the market was possibly undervaluing the share price or putting a high-risk valuation on its earnings.

If the share price is multiplied by the number of shares in issue, the 'capitalisation' of the company is produced — the total value of the issued shares as valued by the market. For Hedgebet this would be:

Issued shares x Market price = 40,000 x £16 = £640,000

The market capitalisation of quoted companies appears in the Monday-morning national newspapers (as there has been no dealing in shares since Friday and therefore space is available in the share information tables). However, it should be remembered that the market in shares is the point at which willing buyers meet willing sellers. Were all the shareholders in a company to try to sell their shares in a company at the same time, the price would be likely to plummet, considerably reducing the market capitalisation of that company.

(d) Dividend yield
One final measure relating to dividend payments is the 'dividend yield'. This is found by dividing the dividend per share by the market price of the share. For Hedgebet, this is:

$$\frac{\text{Dividend per share}}{\text{Market price of share}} = \frac{£1}{£16} = 6.25\%$$

It can be seen that this is exactly one-half of the earnings yield (12.5 per cent), which is to be expected as the dividend payout is one-half of the net income. The dividend yield enables companies to be compared in terms of their payout policy. This can be important, as some companies adopt a policy of regular and constant dividend payouts, and investors come to regard these as dependable income.

The reader should now be able to understand the various columns appearing in a typical share information table. These tables, which appear in the national press, have the following format:

£ High	£ Low	Stock	Closing £ price	+/−	Dividend %	Times covered	Gross yield %	P/E ratio
20	12	Hedgebet	16		6.25	2	12.5	8

7.3 OTHER INFORMATION NEEDS

The potential investor in shares requires not only the information set out in the stock exchange ratios in the previous section, but also more general information. The historical performance of the company and its dividend policy will be studied, as will the Chairman's Statement in the latest available Annual Report. This should give some indication of the future plans and prospects of the company. But company statements should always be evaluated against the environment in which it operates. At the extreme it is not realistic to expect any chairman to forecast bankruptcy in the coming year, even though there may well be a high probability of this event. Factors in the company's environment must also be considered, for these strongly influence a company's prospects. These include its competitors' performance (as a comparative yardstick) and the threats they pose to the company's market position: the overall character and trends in the company's markets; technological changes in its production base; changes in costs, materials, and other factors affecting the company's operations; and the nature of its workforce. Share prices can also be expected to move in respect of industrial unrest, exchange rate fluctuations, changes in interest rates, legislation and the general state of the economy.

The requirements of the individual investor will also be important in the decisions taken. A simple grid can show this (see Fig. 7.1). A person requiring a steady, secure annual income is unlikely to choose the same investment opportunities as a person willing to take risks in order to make large capital gains.

Fig. 7.1

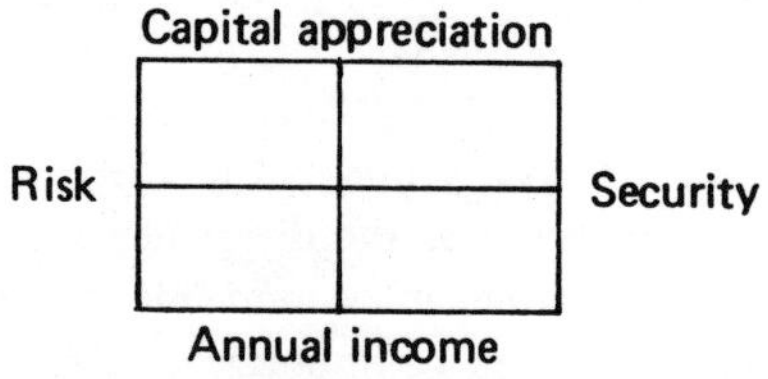

7.4 STOCK EXCHANGE TERMINOLOGY

The stock exchange is the market where stocks and shares are bought and sold, and where, as a result, the prices of stocks and shares are determined. Stockbrokers deal in stocks and shares for clients, and make a living by taking a commission on each transaction they undertake. The stockbroker deals with the public on the one hand and with stockjobbers on the other.

Stockjobbers tend to specialise in one particular section of the market, buying and selling shares on their own behalf and then setting the prices at which they are willing to sell to other jobbers and stockbrokers. The jobber makes his profit on the difference between the purchase and selling price of the stocks and shares he deals in. This is known as the 'jobber's turn'.

Other common terms in the stock market are:

(i) *Bulls.* Who buy stocks and shares hoping they will rise in price and be sold at a profit.

(ii) *Stags.* Who apply for shares which are new to the market hoping to be able to sell them immediately after they receive their allotment and make a profit (because once the shares are available they are popular enough to be sold at a higher level than their original issue price).

(iii) *Bears.* Who are the opposite of bulls. They sell stocks and shares they do not own hoping that their prices will fall by the time they have to be delivered to the purchaser. The *Oxford English Dictionary* suggests the derivation may be from hunters who sell the bear's skin before killing the bear.

8 Capital Investment Appraisal

When a company decides to invest in a new machine or building, or to develop and launch a new product, the consequences are likely to affect the company for a long time. Most companies have limited funds for such capital investment opportunities, and must make the best use of them. These two factors make the investment decision very important. There are limited resources available and the results of their investment will have a long-term impact.

This chapter deals with the basic techniques of investment appraisal, their application in typical investment situations, and with the problems of risk and uncertainty associated with such decisions.

8.1 THE INVESTMENT DECISION

Calculation of the anticipated profitability of an investment is only part of the decision process. The final profit calculation is founded on the various estimates, forecasts and informed guesses that go to provide the cash flow figures. These income and expenditure data for the project will be used to assess its profitability, and to compare it against other investment opportunities open to the firm.

In launching a new product, for instance, a company would have to consider several factors carefully before reaching the stage of assessing its profitability. Marketing research would be intertwined with the investment appraisal. While each market has its own special features, the following are the kinds of questions which will need answering:

    (i)   *The Market*
          What is the size of the market?
          How stable is it?
          How difficult is it for competition to enter the market?
          Who are the customers?
          What are the customers' needs?

(ii) *The Market Growth Potential*
What growth pattern is expected in the market?
What share of the market will the firm attain?
What are the export possibilities?
How long to establish customer acceptance of the product?
What impact will the new product have on existing ones?

(iii) *Product Marketing Potential*
What will customers require of the new product?
How will the new product be promoted?
Will the new product fit into the firm's market image?
What impact will the product have on existing markets?
What kind of service will be required?

(iv) *Internal Factors*
Has the company the necessary competence in this field?
Are raw materials readily available?
What plant facilities will be required for production?
Can existing distribution channels be used?

(v) *Financial Factors*
What capital will be required for fixed assets?
What capital will be required for working capital?
What will be the investment life?
What will be the revenue and costs of the new product?
What will be the cost of raising the capital?

In the light of answers to such questions, the company can start assessing the financial viability of the new venture. The financial calculations depend on the work done by the sales or market research department in forecasting volume, and the manufacturing department in estimating costs and expenses necessary to achieve the physical sales objectives. Given the final figures will involve an aggregation of these estimates and forecasts, they are not likely to have an accuracy of ±10 per cent, therefore there is little point in doing financial calculations to four decimal places. The company will want some assessment of the likely return on investment, but anyone providing an answer such as 'The rate of return on this project will be 18.4725 per cent' is being unrealistically accurate. The mathematical calculations may be correct to four decimal places, but the input data will have such varying degrees of uncertainty that an answer such as 18.4725 per cent is impossibly precise and indeed misleading.

The aim of investment appraisal is to provide management with the basis upon which to take important and far-reaching decisions about where to allocate their limited resources. Part of the job of investment management is to assess the quality of their information and the costs and returns to further information search.

Some of the more common methods of assessing capital investment opportunities are discussed below. But it must be remembered that frequently it is the input data which are critical to the calculations, and not the particular technique adopted for final appraisal.

8.2 METHODS OF APPRAISAL

(a) Payback

The quickest method of assessing a capital investment proposal is to see how long it will take for the project to repay the investment in it. This is the payback method, measuring the time from initial investment to recovery of that amount from the project.

Payback is widely used by companies as a back-up to other appraisal techniques. The reason is that if a company has limited financial resources available, it will be most interested in those projects that give the quickest turnround of its funds. If a company knows it will require a large amount of cash in the near future — having done a detailed cash budget as outlined in Chapter 5 — then only projects that can return their capital before this time may be considered, even though more profitable, but longer term, investments may thereby be rejected.

The example below shows information on three projects together with their payback periods:

	A	B	C
Capital outlay	£1,000	1,000	4,000
Profit before depreciation:			
Year 1	200	800	1,500
2	400	600	1,500
3	600	400	1,500
4	800	200	1,500
5	—	—	1,500
	£2,000	2,000	7,500
Payback period	$2\frac{2}{3}$ years	$1\frac{1}{3}$ years	$2\frac{2}{3}$ years

On the basis of payback, project B is the best, with $1\frac{1}{3}$ years. But if only projects A and C were available, then it would be impossible to distinguish between them on the basis of payback. They both provide a $2\frac{2}{3}$ year payback period.

'Payback' can be used as a coarse sieve to bring up only those proposals worthy of further consideration where cash is a limiting factor both today and in the future. However, the payback period ignores what happens after the payback period. For example, if project A in the fifth year were to provide a pre-depreciation profit of £1,000, this would not alter its assessment under the payback method.

(b) Average rate of return

An alternative is to calculate the average rate of return. If depreciation is assumed to be on the straight-line method, then for projects A and B (assuming a four-year life) depreciation would be £250 each year, and for C (assuming a five-year life) £800 per year. The average rate of return for each project is:

	A	B	C
Total net profit	£1,000	1,000	3,500
Life of project in years	4	4	5
Average annual profit	£250	250	700
Average rate of return	25%	25%	20%

Thus, using average rate of return it would be impossible to choose between projects A and B, as both have a 25 per cent return on capital invested. The reason is because this method effectively assumes a uniform profit over the life of the project. Yet project A has an inverse profit flow to project B.

Thus the average rate of return method ignores the timing of the cash flows, and uses the accounting definition of profit as its basis (after charging the depreciation of the investment). This severely limits its usefulness.

(c) The time value of money: discounting

The main criticism of the two methods of investment appraisal so far illustrated is that they ignore the timing of the cash flows resulting from the investment decision. The average rate of return of projects A and B is 25 per cent. But which one is most acceptable to a company or to an individual? Surely it would be B, because the timing of the income flows is so much better. The greatest income is in the first year in project B, whilst in project A it is in the last year. It is always better to get cash in sooner. Whilst the payback method measures this aspect it is also important to assess the cash flow timing after the payback period for a full appreciation of the investment opportunity.

To bring into the assessment of capital investment proposals the time value of money, all that is required is an understanding of compound interest. Assume that a sum is invested at a fixed rate of interest for a fixed period. The annual interest is added to the initial sum in the first year; in the second year, interest is paid on the initial sum and on the first year's interest, and so on. Interest is paid on interest – it is compounded.

The concept of compound interest is an old one. It was used in Babylon almost four thousand years ago, it was used in Rome and Greece, and for loan interest calculations in the fifteenth and and sixteenth centuries in Europe. Conceptual complexities have never prevented people from making money. Compounding used to be an essential part of school arithmetic. A typical question would be:

What would £1,000 invested at 10% compound interest be worth at the end of five years?

There are two ways of working this problem out. The first is to tackle it the long way round:

Year   1 = £1,000 + £100 = £1,100
2 = £1,100 + £110 = £1,210
3 = £1,210 £ £121 = £1,331
4 = £1,331 + £133 = £1,464
5 = £1,464 + £146 = £1,610

This shows that at the end of five years the £1,000 has become £1,610. There is also a shorter way using the formula

$$\text{Final value} = \text{Amount invested} \ (1 + \text{Rate of interest})^{\text{number of years}}$$
$$= £1,000 \ (1 + 0.1)^5$$
$$= £1,610$$

Using the data in another way, one can say that if the prevailing rate of interest is 10 per cent per annum, then £1,610 in five years' time is worth only £1,000 today. This formula of compound interest can be used to answer questions such as:

What is the present value of £2,000 to be received at the end of two years with a 10% per annum interest rate?

$$\text{Present value} = \frac{\text{Final value}}{(1 + \text{Rate of interest})^{\text{number of years}}}$$
$$= \frac{£2,000}{(1 + 0.1)^2}$$
$$= £1,653$$

This shows that if £1,653 is invested (the present value) at 10 per cent compound interest, it will reach the value of £2,000 at the end of two years. Thus, if a company were offered the certainty of £2,000 in two years' time, and 10 per cent is the ruling rate of interest, it should not pay more than £1,653 today for the opportunity.

The sets of tables in Appendix 3 provide the necessary discount factors to facilitate calculations. To illustrate their application, if a company wishes to provide £1,000 per year for the next five years, to be paid at the end of the year to their best salesman, how much must they invest today to ensure its availability each year? If the interest rate is 10 per cent then, using the 10 per cent columns in the tables at the end of the book, the following discount factors can be obtained:

	10%	Present value
Year 1	0.9091 x £1,000 =	£909.1
2	0.8264 x £1,000 =	£826.4
3	0.7513 x £1,000 =	£751.3
4	0.6830 x £1,000 =	£683.0
5	0.6209 x £1,000 =	£620.9
		£3,790.7

When the discount factors are multiplied by the sum involved (£1,000), this provides the present values which, when totalled, show that £3,790.7 must be invested at 10 per cent interest to provide £1,000 per annum prize. This can be shown in detail:

	Year 1	2	3	4	5	Total
Amounted invested/ balance	£3,790.7	3,169.8	2,486.8	1,735.5	909.0	
Interest at 10%	£379.1	317.0	248.7	173.5	91.0	1,209.3
	£4,169.8	3,486.8	2,735.5	1,909.0	1,000.0	
Salesman prize paid	£1,000.0	1,000.0	1,000.0	1,000.0	1,000.0	5,000.0
Balance carried forward	£3,169.8	2,486.8	1,735.5	909.0	—	

If this example is viewed as a decision to purchase a new machine which will cost £3,790 to instal and will provide £1,000 per year labour and material savings for the company, then it can be seen that this investment will return 10 per cent to the company over the five-year life of the machine, and will recover the capital cost of £3,790.

Note that depreciation is ignored in discounting. It is concerned with the cash outflows and inflows. But the £1,000 per year savings can be translated into straight-line depreciation charge of £758, and 'profit' of £242. The £242 for each year of the five-year life of the machine provides £1,210, which is the same as the interest total £1,209.3 in the original example.

If the savings or profit from the introduction of the new machine had been £1,200 per year, the present value of the five years' cash flows would have been:

Year 1	£1,200 x 09091 = £1,091
2	£1,200 x 08264 = £992
3	£1,200 x 07513 = £902
4	£1,200 x 06830 = £820
5	£1,200 x 06209 = £745
Present value	£4,550

When this £4,550 is compared with the cost of £3,790, it can be seen to be greater by £760. It has a positive net present value when discounted at 10 per cent. This shows that the investment is returning a rate of interest or profit greater than 10 per cent.

To discover the actual rate of return by using the tables it is necessary to choose various discount rates until by trial and error the correct rate is found which brings the present value to equal the cost of £3,790.

Discounting the £1,200 at 15 per cent gives a present value of £4,020 which shows the rate is higher still. Discounting at 20 per cent provides a value of £3,590 which shows the rate is too high. Using 17 per cent gives £3,840 and 18 per cent £3,750. Thus the rate of return of the project is just under 18 per cent.

Where a company has several possible capital investment projects, but limited funds, it will be necessary to rank the choices. If the cost of capital to the firm is known, then this may be used as the discount rate, and any projects that have a negative net present value at this rate can be rejected — they are returning less than the cost of capital and therefore are not profitable.

A further means of ranking within the set of profitable projects is to use a ratio which relates size of return to the amount of investment:

$$\text{Acceptability index} = \frac{\text{Present value of cash flow}}{\text{Capital outlay}}$$

This ratio will highlight the difference, for instance, between a project which costs £2,000 and has a present value of £3,000, and a project which costs £20,000 and has a present value of £21,000. The ratios are 1.5 and 1.05 respectively.

8.3 PRACTICAL APPLICATIONS

Having covered the concept of discounting, we can now consider what information is necessary for its practical application, and what benefits discounted cash flow (DCF) analysis can provide.

The input to the calculations is the cash inflow and outflow associated with the capital investment opportunity. It is really the matching of cash out against cash in over the life of the investment and relating this cash flow back to the initial capital outlay. As has already been shown, depreciation is ignored in discounting. The return from a project is calculated before deducting depreciation charges, and if depreciation has been charged in the accounting process, it must be added back to provide the true cash inflow of the project.

The cash flow that is discounted in a project evaluation is made up as follows:

	£
Income (or savings) in the year	
Less Cost and expenses paid in year	
Taxation paid in year	
Cash flow for year	£ _____

Taxation is an important factor in investment appraisal and must be deducted in the year in which it is paid, not the year in which it is incurred. This applies also to taxation allowances on capital equipment since this is a tax saving which increases the actual cash inflow to the project.

Where a project also requires the provision of working capital to enable operations to begin and continue, then this must be included in the cost of the project.

To illustrate the application of discounted cash flow techniques to investment appraisal, a simple example is provided:

A company has estimated (with some confidence) demand for an item. It must now decide whether it is better to instal one large machine which will meet requirements for the next ten years, but run under capacity for a few years; or to buy a small machine which will cover requirements for five years and then add another small machine which, with the original, will satisfy the remaining five years' demand.

The large machine costs £79,000 and has annual operating costs of £2,000. The small machines cost £50,000 and have operating costs of £1,000 per year. All the machines have estimated lives of ten years.

Which is the better alternative?

The first step is to set out the costs associated with each alternative:

	Two small machines	One large machine
Capital outlay	£50,000	£79,000
Year 1	1,000	2,000
2	1,000	2,000
3	1,000	2,000
4	1,000	2,000
5	1,000	2,000
6	52,000	2,000
7	2,000	2,000
8	2,000	2,000
9	2,000	2,000
10	2,000	2,000
	£115,000	£99,000

If only the aggregate cash outflow were considered, it would be best if the company purchased one large machine immediately. However, the timing of the cash outflows must be considered. If it is assumed that the company has a cost of capital of 10 per cent, then the present values of the two cash flows are:

	Two small machines	One large machine
Initial capital outlay	£50,000	£79,000
Ten years' outgoings discounted at 10%	£36,100	12,300
	£86,100	£91,300

When the present values of the costs are compared, the purchase of two small machines provides the lower sum. As it is cost that is being considered, it is best to minimise the present value and instal two small machines (one of which will still have five years' life at the end of the period). This would also have the added attraction – which cannot be quantified here – of allowing more flexibility to management. Their estimates of demand may turn out to be inaccurate, so that there is no need for a second machine or they may wish to instal the second machine earlier. If, for example, the second machine were added in the fourth year, then the present value of the alternative would be £90,200, which is almost the same as the cost of the larger machine. As long as the second machine is not purchased before year 4, it is best to go for the two small machines. But, as with most investment decisions, attention should be focused not only on the calculations of discounting but on the input data. How certain is management that the estimates are accurate? Some of the methods for improving decision-making under conditions of uncertainty are discussed later in this chapter.

Where a project has a constant stream of income or costs a short cut can be used for calculating the present value. In the case of the large machine there is a constant £2,000 per year cost for the ten years' life of the machine. This has a present value of:

Year		
1	£2,000 x 0.909 =	£1,818
2	£2,000 x 0.826 =	1,652
3	£2,000 x 0.751 =	1,502
4	£2,000 x 0.683 =	1,366
5	£2,000 x 0.621 =	1,242
6	£2,000 x 0.564 =	1,128
7	£2,000 x 0.513 =	1,026
8	£2,000 x 0.467 =	934
9	£2,000 x 0.424 =	848
10	£2,000 x 0.386 =	772
	6.144	£12,288

The £12,288 present value is of a constant annual payment of £2,000. If the discount factors are added they total 6.144, and if £2,000 is multiplied by this it provides £12,288. There are special annuity tables which provide these factors in the case of constant cash flows. They save the tedium of doing the individual calculations. Where these are not at hand and where a calculator is not available it is always simpler to add the discount factors for the relevant number of years and do a single multiplication to obtain the present value.

8.4 THE COST OF CAPITAL

In the above example it was assumed that the company had a cost of capital of 10 per cent. Namely, the cost of raising the finance for the project was 10 per cent; the interest to be paid to the bank to borrow the money. Where a project is to generate income it is essential that it return at least the cost of capital to the company. Otherwise it will be losing money.

Investment proposals can be discounted at the cost of capital rate to see if they have a positive net present value. If so, this indicates that they make a greater return than the cost of providing the finance. This provides a quick coarse sieve, in that projects which cannot produce a positive net present value when discounted at the cost of capital rate need not be considered further. The cost of capital represents the minimum level of return acceptable on investments by a company.

However, the cost of capital for discounting purposes is not necessarily the rate paid to the bank for borrowing. Not even if there is surplus cash in the bank is the cost of capital zero. Companies obtain their funds from a whole series of sources (as shown in Chapter 6) and these all have different costs.

The company will have share capital and reserves – the shareholders' interest, upon which dividends will be paid. There will be loan capital upon which interest must be paid, and other short-term liabilities which have a cost. One method of arriving at the cost of capital is to take the weighted average cost. This involves taking each source of funds, determining its interest cost, and then weighting this cost in proportion to the amount each source makes of the whole.

Another method is to calculate the rate of return that the company is currently making and use this as the minimum acceptance rate for future projects.

There are many theoretical problems in defining the cost of capital, which can be investigated further in the numerous books on capital budgeting and investment appraisal.[1] The intention in this chapter is to make the manager aware that he must have some indication of the cost of capital if full benefit is to be obtained from the use of discounted cash flow analysis.

8.5 RISK AND UNCERTAINTY IN THE INVESTMENT DECISION

All investment decisions are concerned with the future. Capital is invested in a project now for future returns, so there is always some degree of uncertainty associated with the cash flows upon which the decisions are based. Except in very unusual circumstances, it is impossible to be certain what the situation will be five years after an investment decision is made. This applies particularly in competitive markets. If the input data to investment decisions are poor, then the chances of making adequate decisions are greatly reduced.

While there is no formula for ensuring good investment decisions by companies, there are several ways in which the base information can be presented to management so as to provide a better foundation upon which to take the decision.

(a) Three-level estimates

In the production of any cash flow for an investment appraisal, those concerned will have had to make assumptions in several areas, some within the company's control, some external to it. For example:

(i) the level of demand (including likely competitive responses);
(ii) the cost of materials;
(iii) the price to be charged;
(iv) the product life cycle;
(v) the capital required;
(vi) the working capital required.

With these factors, and many more, underlying a cash flow forecast, if they were to present a single cash flow proposal, this would conceal the degree and range of estimation. More is required for a good decision.

One simple way to provide more information about the proposed investment is to produce three cash flows: one for the best conditions likely to prevail under the project, one for the worst conditions, and a third for the most likely outcome. These can then be set out as:

	Best	Most likely	Worst
Capital outlay			
Annual cash flow			

When these are discounted either for the rate of return or the net present value, they provide a better overall feel for the project, and the possible payments associated with it. The assumptions as to the best and worst outcomes of the investment must be as realistic as possible in order for full benefit to be achieved.

If the return on the project may be between 25 and 8 per cent, then management can set this against the cost of raising the funds. If the cost of capital is 12 per cent, then they can weigh the risk of the project only returning 8 per cent in their decision. If the firm cannot under any circumstances afford a return of 8 per cent, it can be rejected as too risky, even though there is a possibility of returns as high as 25 per cent.

(b) Sensitivity analysis

A further way of improving the data is to see which factors have the greatest impact on its success. This is known as sensitivity analysis. For example, if the investment is for a new product, and the critical factor is uncertainty of demand, the investment proposal can be framed to highlight this fact, and show a series of cash flows and returns for the project at differing levels of demand. For example, the information may be as follows, showing different demand patterns and totals:

		Year 1	2	3	4	Total
Capital outlay		£100,000				£100,000
Demand (Units)	(A)	300	500	300	100	1,200
	(B)	400	600	400	150	1,550
	(C)	500	800	800	200	2,300
	(D)	600	1,000	800	100	2,500

The cash flow for each demand pattern (in £'000) at a price of £100 per unit, is

		Year 1	2	3	4
Demand pattern	(A)	30	50	30	10
	(B)	40	60	40	15
	(C)	50	80	80	20
	(D)	60	100	80	10

The net present values of these cash flows when discounted at 10 per cent are:

Demand pattern	(A)	(B)	(C)	(D)
Net present value discounted at 10%	(−£2,000)	£26,000	£85,000	£104,000

With this information management is in a better position to assess the proposal. Demand is the most sensitive factor in the eventual profitability of the project, and a range of expected demand patterns are shown together with their present values and returns.

This sort of analysis can also be used effectively where a machine installation is considered. Different life expectancies can be used to assess the viability of the investment – i.e. what happens to the return on the investment if the machine lasts only for two years rather than five.

With the Internal Rate of Return (IRR) – the rate at which inflows equal outflows – no more information is provided than with the NPV, and there are problems associated with its calculation at high levels, so it is best ignored for practical purposes.

(c) Expected value

It is also possible to incorporate simple statistical techniques into the investment proposal. One very useful technique involves calculating 'expected value'. An example will illustrate its use:

	Demand	Cash flow	Probability	Expected value
Year 1	300 units	£30,000	0.3	£9,000
	400 units	40,000	0.4	16,000
	500 units	55,000	0.2	11,000
	600 units	70,000	0.1	7,000
			1.0	£43,000

The possible demand levels in the first year together with the cash flows are set out in the table, and against each of these possible outcomes is a probability of occurrence. The sales manager is asked to estimate the probability of the occurrence of each demand level, and in this case he has estimated that there is a 30 per cent chance of 300 units, 40 per cent of 400, 20 per cent of 500 and a 10 per cent chance of 600 units. Note that the total probability for each year must aggregate to 1. The probability of occurrence is multiplied by the outcome and the results totalled to provide the expected value. In this example the expected cash flow for the first year is £43,000.

This figure of £43,000 is more useful than a straightforward average which would show a value of

$$\frac{£30,000 + £40,000 + £55,000 + £70,000}{4} = £48,750$$

as it takes into account the estimated likelihood of the event — in this case the cash flow for each level of demand. It is also better than just taking the most likely (the one with the highest probability of occurrence) — of £40,000, because it takes into account the significant probability that it will be more or less than this amount.

It is possible to calculate the expected cash flows for each year of a project's life, and use these in the discounting calculations. The resulting figures are better than the single cash flow estimates normally produced. The range of possible outcomes is covered, not just the average or most likely. Thus this method gives a better appreciation of the project's potential.

(d) Monte Carlo simulation

A further refinement is to apply probability analysis, for which it is necessary to have access to computing facilities. The first step is to outline the key factors upon which eventual profitability depends, as illustrated with sensitivity analysis earlier in this chapter. With a new product these factors would mainly involve cost, price and volume. With a labour-saving machine investment they might be capital cost, savings and machine life.

Having isolated these factors, probabilities are estimated for their possible outcomes. For example, consider the following data on an investment proposal:

Working capital		Annual returns		Annual running costs	
£'000	Prob. %	£'000	Prob. %	£'000	Prob. %
10–20	10	5–10	25	3–6	5
20–30	60	10–15	50	6–9	15
30–40	25	15–20	20	9–12	70
40–50	5	20–25	5	12–15	10

This can be graphed either as a cumulative probability curve or as a frequency distribution, as illustrated in Fig. 8.1.

Fig. 8.1

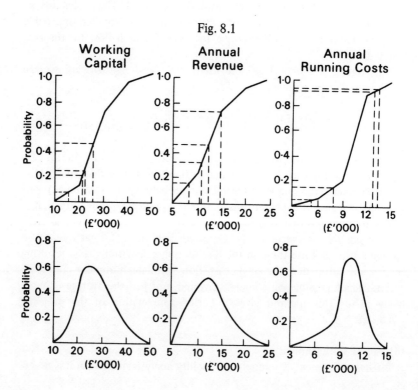

The data in these graphs can be used to provide an estimate of the likely range of outcomes of the investment proposal. This process is commonly called Monte Carlo simulation because a large number of random samples are taken (within the given probability distributions) before being processed into a cash flow, and discounted to provide either net present values or rates of return. In Fig. 8.1 it is possible to use random numbers to choose points from each of the three factors and combine them to provide a cash flow. If it is assumed that the cumulative probability curve graph has a vertical axis divided into 100 points, then random numbers can be used to choose outcomes from each graph. For example, if the random numbers are

A	B	C	D
20 74 94	22 15 93	45 44 16	04 32 03

then these can be used for the three factors as follows:

		Working capital	Annual revenue	Annual running costs
Random choice	(A)	20 = £22,000	74 = £14,000	94 = £13,500
	(B)	22 = £23,000	15 = £6,000	93 = £13,000
	(C)	45 = £26,000	44 = £12,000	16 = £8,000
	(D)	04 = £14,000	32 = £10,500	03 = £4,500

The monetary values are found from the cumulative probability graph and shown by the dotted lines. Each one of the combinations will provide a different present value and rate of return, and if sufficient random samples are taken, a comprehensive picture of the likely outcomes of the investment will be available. This can be used by management to decide whether or not to accept the proposal and allocate capital to its initiation.

The graphs of frequency distribution can be used in the same manner. In the sampling method the choice is weighted by the probability of its occurrence. Thus, more use would be made of the running costs between £9,000 and £12,000 than of any other level because these have the highest probability of occurring.

The use of probability analysis does not solve the problem of the investment decision for management. It merely provides better information or insight into the possible outcomes, or the ranges of potential profitability, of the project. The manager must still apply his knowledge, experience and ability to finding the best solution. And this will include an assessment of the quality of the data input, and of the reliability and motives of the estimating sources.

9 Introduction to Management Accounting

It is often thought that costing systems exist to provide a basis for pricing decisions. The cost of a product is certainly important in setting prices, but this is by no means its only use. The main purpose of a costing system is to enable management to control operations, to plan for future growth and profitability. Cost accounting has wide application in all aspects of management. A firm can rarely be effectively run if the various elements of cost and their behaviour are not understood and monitored. Nor can planning be undertaken without knowledge of how the various costs will react to changes in the level of operations, and how they will affect profitability. The simple formula:

$$\text{Profit} = \text{Revenue} - \text{Costs}$$

highlights the importance of cost. Costing systems are designed to give management the ability to control costs and to understand how the various costs of their operations react to changes in volume or in relation to other factors. First we introduce the different types of cost, and then go on to consider various costing systems.

9.1 TYPES OF COST

There are many ways of classifying costs, and many different bits of terminology to describe those costs. This chapter and Chapter 10 use, as far as possible, common and simple terms in outlining cost behaviour and cost systems. Every manager is recommended to visit the management accountant in his firm and discover what methods of costing are used and what terminology is adopted. The management accountant is employed to provide management with information for decision-making. If managers cannot understand the methods used to provide the information, then the system is of little benefit, and the accountant is failing to communicate with those he is intended to service.

One basic classification of cost relates to the time scale. If an expenditure is made in the current financial year, but will have benefits in future years, then it may be spread over a number of years as a charge in the Profit and Loss Account. The expenditure is 'capitalised'. Thus, if a machine is expected to have a life of at least five years, the accountant may spread the expense over five years' accounts. The total amount of expenditure is capitalised and written off over a number of years. This applies not only to physical assets, but may also be used for such expenditures as advertising and research and development where the benefits of current expenditure will accrue in future periods.

If an item is not capitalised, then it will be treated as a revenue expense or an income charge. That is, it will be written off in the accounts for the year in which it was incurred. For example, routine maintenance to keep the firm's machinery working efficiently will tend to be written off in the year in which it is undertaken.

The manner in which various expenditures are treated as either capital or revenue is important in that the decision will have a direct impact on the profit shown in the firm's accounts. This was shown in earlier chapters dealing with financial reports. There is rarely one correct approach to the decision, and much will rely on the current practice in the firm concerned. In major companies changes will be noticed and commented upon by the financial analysts.

Having decided in which year an expense belongs, one can move to a consideration of the elements of costs. These can be illustrated as in Fig. 9.1.

Fig. 9.1

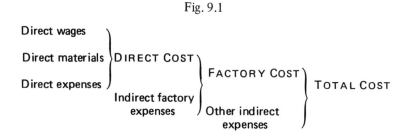

The accountant should always try to provide management with a realistic cost upon which to base current control activities and budgets for future profitability. But no single correct way of calculating 'the cost' of a product has yet been devised — though there are indeed incorrect ways. Each firm will have its own system of cost data. This diversity underlines the need for managers to discover from their own accountant which approach is used in their own firm. The problems in ascertaining a cost can be shown by taking each element of cost in turn.

The direct costs of a product are those costs which can be indisputably placed against units of output. Direct wages are wages paid to employees on the shop floor physically to produce the products. It may be thought that there are no problems in discovering the true wage cost of production. There will be job cards to show which workers did what and when. But even if these are accurate and reliable, what about the problem of overtime and bonus payments? Must the customer who purchases products made whilst workers were on overtime pay more for them? And how are PAYE, insurance, holiday pay and training to be treated? So the accountant must make assumptions to provide management with the direct labour content and cost of units of output. There is no readily available and indisputable direct wage cost.

Direct materials are those materials used in production. But, as illustrated in Chapter 3, there are many methods of valuing materials and charging them out to production. The actual figure for direct materials cost will depend on whether LIFO, FIFO, average cost or some other method of stock valuation has been adopted. The figure shown in the manufacturing account of the firm for materials used in production is developed from certain basic assumptions and estimates made by the accountant, and in order to make use of that information the manager must understand what these are.

Together with the direct expenses associated with the physical production of the goods to be sold there are other indirect expenses. These are expenses that cannot be assigned to units of output. They will consist of such items as management salaries, insurance, rates, interest on loans, depreciation and research.

Since indirect expenses cannot be properly assigned to production or sales, they must be allocated in some manner by the accountant. Whilst there are many accepted methods of allocation, there is no single agreed method that can be used to provide 'the' correct cost data on a product. For example, any one of the various methods of depreciation outlined in Chapter 3 could be applied, and each would tend to provide a different loading of indirect cost to units of output, but none could be said to be incorrect. It is a matter of judgement and opinion. In order to discover the cost of a department or section in a works, it will be necessary for there to be rule-of-thumb allocations of overall indirect expenses. These allocation methods will be discussed later in this chapter, and some of the problems associated with them dealt with in Chapter 10.

It is possible to split the various costs of a business into two major parts — the variable costs and the fixed costs. Variable costs are those costs which change in direct proportion to output. For example, direct material and wages are variable costs, in that if the material content of a product is £10 and the labour for assembling and packing is £20, then for each unit there will be a cost of £30. If 100 units are produced the cost will be £3,000, if 400 are produced, £12,000, and so on. The cost varies in direct proportion to the number produced. A fixed cost is one which does not change in relation to variations in output or sales. The rent and rates of a factory will remain constant whatever the level of output achieved up to the point where a new factory is built or an extension added to the existing one to cater for the increased volume.

Fig. 9.2

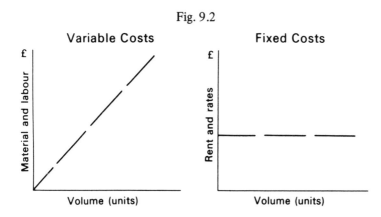

It is possible to graph these costs as illustrated in Fig. 9.2 and to combine them into a graph showing the total cost (assuming there are no other expenses) at various levels of volume (Fig. 9.3).

Fig. 9.3

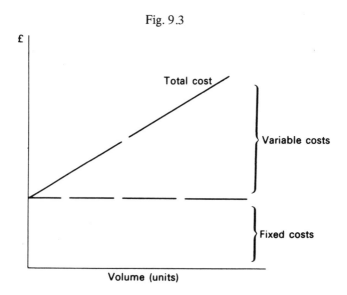

This approach will be developed in Chapter 10, which discusses break-even analysis and marginal costing.

In any firm there will be costs which cannot be neatly split into a variable and a fixed element, and investigation will have to be made as to how they behave. In many firms even labour cannot be taken as a truly variable cost as the firm must keep on skilled employees even if for short periods there is little for them to do. Experienced or skilled labour can rarely be hired and fired as production fluctuations dictate, and therefore labour may be treated as, at least in part, a fixed cost.

Managers should not be lulled into thinking 'fixed' costs are not reducible. They are only fixed in relation to volume, and there are usually ways in which they can, at a pinch, be reduced by managerial action.

One final classification of costs is the differentiation between product costs and period costs. Product costs are those that relate to the production of the goods being sold by the firm, and will consist of all costs incurred in producing the goods to be sold. Thus, product costs will include all direct costs, such as labour and materials, and all other costs and expenses that can be directly related to the production of goods in the firm. Period costs are costs which relate to a particular time or period rather than to the physical production of units. These costs will be set against the revenue generated in the period in which they are incurred, and not allocated to units of production. It will depend upon which type of costing system is adopted by a firm as to which costs are classified as period costs rather than product costs. The more common types of costing systems are described in the following sections of this chapter.

9.2 FULL OR ABSORPTION COSTING

Under full or absorption costing the costs for a period are related to the production of that period. That is, all factory costs, whether they are fixed or variable, are applied to the number of units produced. The other expenses such as general administration, financial costs and selling expenses are set against revenue in the Profit and Loss Account for the period, but are not allocated to units of production.

This method of costing provides a stock valuation at 'full cost'. Indirect expenses are included in the stock valuation. Although full costing is still in wide use, there are several problems connected with its application. These are illustrated in the introduction to marginal costing in Chapter 10. In brief, the major difficulties are as follows:

(i) In concentrating on factory costs, full costing ignores major expenses such as selling, distribution, financial and administration costs.

(ii) As a result of (i) above, management often has to use gross profit margins rather than net profit margin, particularly in the pricing decision. This can be seriously misleading.

(iii) As the cost of a unit of production is found by dividing the total factory cost by the number of units produced, there is no firm cost for management to use. As volume changes, so will the 'cost' per unit.

(iv) Following from (iii) above, full costing is of little benefit to management in forward planning of profitable growth.

(v) As a result of using full costing it is possible for management to reject profitable opportunities to use spare capacity. (See Chapter 10 for a detailed explanation of this.)

9.3 OVERHEAD APPLICATION

In any firm there will be a major section of costs that cannot be assigned to products or departments. These are the indirect costs or overheads. The accountant is often expected to provide cost details that include the indirect costs, and he must therefore spread or apply these overheads. There are many ways of doing this, but only the most common are illustrated here.

The simplest method is to take the total overhead figure and divide it by the number of units produced. But this assumes that each unit is identical and should share equally in the indirect costs. Where a company is manufacturing many products this is unlikely to be the case.

A very common method is to apply the overheads in relation to the direct labour hours or costs for the various products or units produced. Where labour is the critical factor in the operation, this is a useful basis for applying overheads. The rate can be calculated as follows:

$$\frac{\text{Estimated overhead}}{\text{Estimated direct labour cost for period}}$$

or

$$\frac{\text{Estimated overhead}}{\text{Estimated direct labour hours for period}}$$

The rate of application is then used on whichever denominator has been used in the equation. When labour cost is used as the denominator, there may be problems where employees on different pay scales do the same work. For instance, if overheads are recovered on the basis of 100 per cent on labour costs, then a skilled man at £4 per hour will incur £4 per hour indirect costs on the job in which he is involved, while an unskilled man at

£2 per hour doing the same job, perhaps producing one unit of output, will have only £2 indirect cost applied.

It is also possible to calculate machine hour rates to charge overheads to production. In this case the equation becomes:

$$\frac{\text{Estimated overhead}}{\text{Estimated machine hours}}$$

This method is particularly applicable in machine shops, where different rates will be calculated for each machine or group of machines. However, there are difficulties in calculating machine hour rates and in keeping records of machine hours worked on individual jobs or units, and therefore application on the basis of labour tends to be more commonly used since it is simpler.

9.4 STANDARD COSTING

Standard costing has long been used to provide control of operations. Effectively it provides a standard by estimating what costs should be under normal operating efficiency. With a predetermined standard it is easier to compare and control actual operation costs. It can quickly show where problems are arising and which manager or department is responsible. Actual costs are compared against the standards and the resulting variances are analysed to show which factor is the source of the variance. If actual costs are higher than standard, this may be the result of material price rises, or because more of it has been used than expected.

Standards may be set for all elements of cost — material, labour and overheads — and with varying degrees of rigour. For example, the standard may be based on historic experience, and may not change from period to period. This is not a particularly challenging standard, but does provide a common base for performance and efficiency measurement. However, as this standard may become out of date, it is not of real use in cost control. At the other extreme it is possible to set an ideal standard, that can only be attained if everything works perfectly and there are no problems. Such a challenging standard (perhaps linked to an incentive payment system) may produce more effort from employees, but it can result in these standards being disregarded as unattainable. Another tactic is to define a standard which can be attained with normal operating efficiency and effort, lower than the ideal but requiring an effort to achieve. This last standard is the most commonly used. The employees are given a standard which they can attain with full effort, and one which will be useful in comparing actual performance with expected results. The motivational implications of standards are discussed in Chapter 11, which deals with budgetary control.

In setting standards for materials those concerned should be involved. It is not normally possible for the accountant to do this by himself. The main function concerned will be purchasing, and they will be accountable for at least part of any variances between actual and standard materials costs. The standard will be based on an estimate of material prices in the coming period. Actual prices will then be compared with these standards to assess the efficiency of purchasing as well as the appropriateness of the standard.

The standard cost of materials will also depend upon expected use during the period. It will be necessary to split the overall material cost variance into its two component parts, price and use. The resulting price and usage variances are illustrated in the example below:

To produce 100 units of a product, the standard cost of material is £2,000, the standard amount of materials 1,000 lb and the standard price £2. The actual cost of producing 100 units was found to be £2,640 in using 1,200 lb of material at a cost of £2.2.

Standard cost = 1,000 lb at £2 =	£2,000
Actual cost = 1,200 lb at £2.2 =	£2,640
Total adverse variance	(£640)

Price variance
Actual quantity of materials multiplied by price difference
(1,200)   x   (£2 – £2.2) = (£240)

Usage variance
Standard price multiplied by usage difference
(£2)   x   (1,000 – 1,200) = (£400)
£640

The price variance is found by taking the actual quality of materials and using the difference between the actual and the standard price to calculate the amount of the overall variance resulting from the price change in the material used. This variance can be used by the purchasing department to assess their ability to get the lowest prices.

The usage variance is found by taking the standard price and the difference between the actual and the standard quantity. This variance can be used by the factory manager to help assess his production efficiency.

The same procedure is followed for analysing labour variances. A standard payment rate is set for the work and the standard time allotted for its completion. The overall variance can then be split into the price, or rate, variance and the usage or efficiency variance. An example is provided below:

The standard for a unit is 10 hours at £2 per hour	= £20
The actual for a unit was 9 hours at £2.5 per hour	= £22.5
Total adverse variance	(£2.5)

Rate variance
Actual hours multiplied by rate difference
    (9)   x   (£2 − £2.5)   = (£4.5)

Efficiency variance
Standard rate multiplied by time difference
    (£2)   x   (10 − 9)   = £2.0
                                          (£2.5)

These types of variance can be illustrated in the form of a diagram (Fig. 9.4). This clearly illustrates the favourable variance from completing the work in one hour better than standard, and the adverse variance of paying more than the standard rate for those nine hours' work. Had the actual time taken been eleven hours, then the diagram would have appeared as Fig. 9.5.

It can be seen that the right-hand corner square could be taken in either of the two variances. It could either be taken as part of the rate variance to

Fig. 9.4

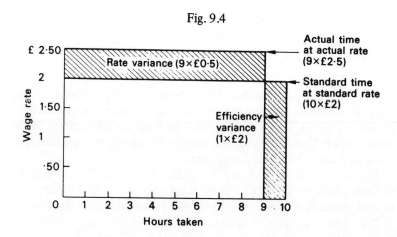

Fig. 9.5

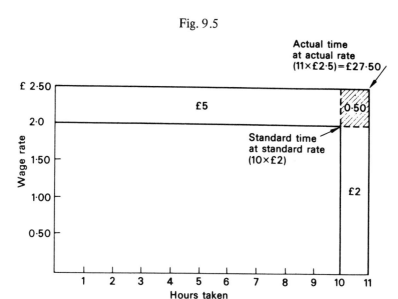

make this £5.50, or in the efficiency variance to make this £2.50. The convention is that it appears as part of the rate variance, but there is always that area of dispute in fixing responsibility for the adverse variance.

In setting overhead standards one must define some level of activity upon which to base the rate for applying the overheads. Management requires similar information concerning overheads to that used with labour and materials. Is the variance due to the fact that more than expected was spent, or due to a different level of activity than was used in setting the standard? Where overheads represent a significant proportion of costs in an operation, it is important that they be controlled and monitored just as regularly as the direct costs. The method by which overheads are applied may be on the basis of labour, materials or machine hours and on an estimate of activity in the coming period. To get full benefit from standard costing it is necessary to split overheads into the part that varies in relation to changes in output, and that which remains fixed — a variable overhead and a fixed overhead component. Often there will have to be an arbitrary allocation, but analysis of the nature of overheads can itself be beneficial.

In the example below, the variable overheads are applied on the basis of direct labour hours. That is, an estimate has been made of the future level of variable overheads. This has then been related to an estimate of the future level of activity, so as to obtain the labour hour rate necessary to

146

recover those overheads:

The estimated variable overheads for the period are £25,000, and the estimated hours to be worked are 12,500, which produce a standard rate of £2 per hour. Actual variable overheads for the period were £33,000 and the actual hours worked were 15,000 to produce the standard number of units of output.

Spending variance

(The actual variable overhead rate is

$$\frac{£33,000}{15,000} = £2.2 \text{ per hour})$$

Actual hours worked multiplied by rate difference

(15,000)   x   (£2 – £2.2) =   (£3,000)

Efficiency variance

Standard rate multiplied by hours difference

(£2)   x   (12,500 – 15,000) =   (£5,000)

                                      (£8,000)

Check

Actual variable overhead	£33,000
Standard variable overhead	£25,000
Overall adverse variance	(£8,000)

Here the variance between the actual and the standard amount of variable overheads is found by subtracting the actual overhead rate (£2.2 per hour) from the standard rate and multiplying by the actual hours worked. The procedure is similar for all variance analysis. The efficiency variance here is calculated in the same manner as for the labour efficiency variance. The actual and standard hours worked are related to the standard hourly rate (£2). These variances show that the overall adverse variance of £8,000 is divided between overspending and exceeding standard hours worked in production.

Finally, fixed overheads are likely to remain constant despite fluctuations in volume around a normal level of activity. If a unit cost for these is required, then the higher the volume of output the lower the amount each unit will bear of overall fixed costs, and thus the lower the unit cost. The accountant is faced with the task of presenting an acceptable standard cost, despite monthly variations in volume. So it is necessary to decide upon some 'normal' level of activity to provide a rate at which fixed overheads are applied to units of output. The level of activity to use is a matter of judgement. One level of 'normal' activity might be that which the factory is expected to average over the next few years. Alternatively the estimated level of activity for the coming year may be used.

The chosen level of activity is then used to produce an overhead rate. Thus, if fixed overheads for the period are estimated at £20,000 and direct labour hours at 10,000 then a rate of £2 per direct labour hour can be used. Otherwise the £20,000 may be related to any other element that is considered effective in applying fixed overheads. If the firm works only 9,000 hours but incurs fixed overheads of £25,000, the variances are calculated as follows:

Standard fixed overheads £20,000; actual £25,000
Standard hours to be worked 10,000; actual 9,000

Actual fixed overhead applied (9,000 x £2)	= £18,000
Actual fixed overheads incurred	= £25,000
Overall variance	(£7,000)

Expenditure variance
Standard overheads less actual overheads

(£20,000)	–	(£25,000)	= (£5,000)

Volume variance
Standard rate multiplied by hours difference

(£2)	x	(9,000 – 10,000)	= (£2,000)
			(£7,000)

These variances show the impact of fixed overheads exceeding the standard and of the number of hours worked falling below standard. They combine to explain the overall actual variance of £7,000.

It is possible to develop variance analysis further to show an efficiency variance and a capacity variance for the fixed overheads. The efficiency variance shows the gain or loss from the actual output being below or above the standard time allowed, and the capacity variance deals with the change in the unit overhead cost due to changes in the level of activity.

9.5 INTERPRETATION OF VARIANCES

The manager should first discover what variances are calculated in his firm under standard costing and, most important, how they are calculated. The above examples show in broad outline the type of variance analysis that can be undertaken, but every firm has its own methods and terminology. If the principle has been understood, then this can be related to the individual firm.

Not all standard costing systems will use the same basis as the examples shown above. Not only may the method of calculation be different, but also the method of presentation. It is quite usual to see the standard costing variances expressed in ratio or percentage terms. For example, the labour rate variance may be shown as:

$$\frac{\text{Actual hours at actual rate}}{\text{Actual hours at standard rate}} \times 100 = \%$$

The presentation of variances in management reports does not of itself ensure better control of costs. Control can only be achieved by in-depth investigation of the causes of the variances. In such a study it is often useful to separate those variances that are beyond the control of management from those which clearly are controllable. For example, if all suppliers of the firm's raw materials have increased their prices by 10 per cent, then there is little point in spending a lot of time investigating the resulting materials price variance. It is beyond the control of the purchasing department – though they might try to get the product redesigned, or look for a substitute.

Management must also decide what size of variance is worth attention. If every variance is investigated, this will waste time and perhaps discredit the whole control system by annoying the managers concerned. Some level has to be set at which a study will be undertaken to see why the variance arose and what should be done about it. What this level is will depend upon the type of firm and its size. For example, a level of ±10 per cent could be set, or all variances over £500, beyond which a full investigation will be made, with the participation of those responsible.

Standard costing variances seldom provide the answer to questions. They merely show that the questions should be asked. But standard costing systems provide a basis for sound and speedy control. Problem areas are quickly pinpointed, so that management can take action before it is too late. Standard costing also enables each key manager to see what impact his function has on the success of the firm, and enables regular detailed comparison of standard with actual performance.

9.6 PROCESS COSTING

Where a firm produces a continuous flow of product moving from one process to another, rather than individual units, process costing is used. Process costing follows the progress of the product from its introduction into the production system via the various processes, into saleable form. It is used in process industries such as chemicals, textiles and foods. The intention is to identify the cost of production at each stage in the overall production process so as to show productive efficiency, spoilage and waste.

To operate process costing, the factory is divided into separate departments or processes, each responsible for one particular activity. For example, in a textile firm one department may card, one dye, one spin, and one weave the cloth. Each department has its own identifiable costs — material, labour and indirect expenses — and these are recorded against production as the product moves to the next stage in the process. Quite often standards are set for each department, thus allowing the use of standard costing in the process flow. The finished stock of one process moves to become the raw material of the next until the product is ready for sale to customers.

Under process costing, great attention is paid to loss, scrap, spoil and general wastage. Normal losses can be estimated and abnormal loss highlighted.

With continuous flow production there is the problem of valuing work-in-progress for accounting purposes. One widely used method is to calculate the equivalent production and allocate costs on this basis. The equivalent production is found by studying the process to see how far towards completion are the units. If 1,000 units are 50 per cent completed, then this is taken to be the same as 500 units fully complete.

In process costing there are often joint products — two or more products are produced from the same process. In these circumstances some basis has to be set for allocating portions of the initial raw material cost between these products. There may also be by-products, produced incidentally as the main products are processed. Again, some estimate of the cost to be set against these by-products will have to be made by the accountant.

9.7 CONTRACT COSTING

Contract costing is the opposite in many ways to process costing. With contract costing each contract or job has its own account, and costs are collected against this. This form of costing is particularly applicable to civil engineering and construction work, but also widely used in heavy engineering — ships, large transformers, etc.

Each job or contract is assigned an accounts code or number and all work done on that contract is charged against that code. All materials, whether issued from stores or specially purchased, bear the number of the contract; all labour and, where possible, all indirect costs are also set against the particular contract.

By recording the costs associated with a particular contract in this manner, management has a flow of information with which to monitor progress against planned performance, and to see what profit has been returned at the conclusion of each contract.

10 Contribution Analysis

In the previous chapter various types of costing systems were examined. In this chapter marginal costing is explained and illustrated. Its principal advantage is that it enables information to be presented in readily understandable form for pricing and make-or-buy decisions.

10.1 THE PROBLEM OF OVERHEAD ALLOCATION

Consider a firm's budget for the coming year:

Budgeted sales	1,000 units at a price of £22	£22,000

Budgeted direct costs:		
Materials (£5 per unit)	£5,000	
Labour (£4 per unit)	£4,000	
Other (£3 per unit)	£3,000	£12,000

Budgeted indirect costs:		
Administration expenses	£4,000	
Financial charges (depreciation, etc)	£3,000	£7,000
		£19,000

Cost per unit (£19,000/1,000) = £19
Profit per unit (£22 − £19) = £3
Budgeted profit for year (£3 x 1,000) = £3,000

The company expects to make £3 profit per unit as the difference between the full cost per unit (as defined under absorption costing in Chapter 9) and the selling price of £22, and produce £3,000 overall profit for the year at the budgeted level of sales.

If the company had prepared budgets for an output and sale of 800 units of the product, then the figures would have been:

Sales income: 800 units at a price £22   £17,600

Budgeted direct costs:

Materials	£4,000	
Labour	£3,200	
Other	£2,400	£9,600

Cost per unit (£16,600/800)   = £20.75
Profit per unit (£22 – £22.75)   = £1.25
Budgeted profit for the year   = £1,000

Now suppose the company originally budgeted to produce and sell 800 units and achieved production and sales of 1,000 units. In calculating the profitability they might do the following sum:

Budgeted profit per unit (£1.25) × 1,000 units sold
= Profit of £1,250

So the profit for the year appears to be £1,250. But the earlier budget for 1,000 units showed a profit of £3,000. So there are two substantially different profit figures for making and selling 1,000 units of the product. Which is correct, the £1,250 or the £3,000?

Clearly, it must be the £3,000 which comes from the budget to produce and sell 1,000 of the product. The reason for the differences in the two profit figures is the indirect costs. These are fixed in so far as they do not vary whether the company produces 800 or 1,000 units. The administration salaries, rent and rates, etc., will still be £4,000 and the financial charges will still be £3,000 at 800 units output and sale.

When the company calculated the cost per unit at 800 units output and sale it assumed that each unit would bear 1/800th of the £7,000 indirect costs, or £8.75 per unit. Yet when the company actually achieves output and sale of 1,000 units, each unit should bear only 1/1000th of the £7,000, or £7 per unit. The same cost is spread over more units.

Thus, in taking the £8.75 per unit indirect cost allocation into the calculations, each unit is having to bear £1.75 too much indirect costs (£8.75 – £7). If this £1.75 is multiplied by the 1,000 units it provides the £1,750 difference between the £1,250 and the £3,000 profits.

The company using the 800 unit budget data has been overcharging each unit for the recovery of its total indirect expenses. It has been over-recovering the indirect expenses. This would be shown in the accountant's

153

report as:

Profit from sale of 1,000 units	£1,250
Overrecovery of indirect expenses	£1,750
Profit for the year	£3,000

Where a company is using full or absorption costing to provide a unit cost and profit figure, profitability will be overstated if the budget is not attained, and understated when it is exceeded. Indirect expenses will have been under- or overrecovered, and allowance must be made for this in calculating real profitability.

As a further example of problems that can be created by the allocation of indirect or overhead expenses and costs to units of output, the following dialogue is reprinted from the *Lybrand Journal*:

In discussing the costs incident to various types of operations, the analogy was drawn of the Restaurant which adds a rack of peanuts to the counter, intending to pick up a little additional profit in the usual course of business. This analogy was attacked as an over-simplification. However, the accuracy of the analogy is evident when one considers the actual problem faced by the Restauranteur (Joe) as revealed by his Accountant-Efficiency-Expert:

EFF EX: Joe, you said you put in these peanuts because some people ask for them but do you realise what this rack of peanuts is *costing you?*

JOE: It ain't gonna cost. 'Sgonna be a profit. Sure I hadda pay $25 for a fancy rack to holda bags, but the peanuts cost 6c a bag but I sell 'em for 10. Figger I sell 50 bags a week to start. It'll take 12½ weeks to cover the cost of the rack. After that I gotta clear profit of 4c a bag. The more I sell, the more I make.

EFF EX: That is an antiquated and completely unrealistic approach, Joe. Fortunately, modern accounting procedures permit a more accurate picture which reveals the complexities involved.

JOE: Huh?

EFF EX: To be precise, those peanuts must be integrated into your entire operation and be allocated their appropriate share of business overhead. They must share a proportionate part of your expenditures for rent, heat, light, equipment depreciation, decorating, salaries for waitresses, cook. . . .

JOE: The *cook*? What's he gotta do wit'a peanuts? He don' even know I got em!

EFF EX: Look, Joe, the cook is in the kitchen, the kitchen prepares the food, the food is what brings people in here, and the people ask to buy peanuts. *That's* why you must charge a portion of the cook's wages, as well as a part of your own salary, to peanut sales. This sheet contains a carefully calculated cost analysis which indicates the peanut operation should pay exactly $1,278 per year toward these general overhead costs.

JOE: The peanuts? $1,278 a year for overhead? The nuts?

EFF EX: It's really a little more than that. You also spend money each week to have the windows washed, to have the place swept out in the mornings, keep soap in the washroom and provide free cokes to the police. That raises the total to $1,313 per year.

JOE (*Thoughtfully*): But the peanut salesman said I'd make money . . . put 'em on the end of the counter, he said . . . and get 4c a bag profit . . .

EFF EX (*With a sniff*): He's not an accountant. Do you actually know what the portion of the counter occupied by the peanut rack is worth to you?

JOE: Ain't worth nothing — no stool there . . . just a dead spot at the end.

EFF EX: The modern cost picture permits no dead spots. Your counter contains 60 square feet and your counter business grosses $15,000 a year. Consequently, the square foot of space occupied by the peanut rack is worth $250 per year. Since you have taken that area away from general counter use, you must charge the value of the space to the occupant.

JOE: You mean I gotta add *$250 a year more* to the peanuts?

EFF EX: Right. That raises their share of the general operating costs to a grand total of $1,563 per year. Now then, if you sell 50 bags of peanuts per week, these allocated costs will amount to 60c per bag.

JOE: WHAT?

EFF EX: Obviously, to that must be added your purchase price of 6c per bag, which brings the total to 66c. So you see by selling peanuts at 10c per bag you are losing 56c on every sale.

JOE: Somethin's crazy!

EFF EX: Not at all! Here are the *figures*. They prove your peanuts operation cannot stand on its own feet.

JOE (*Brightening*): Suppose I sell *lotsa* peanuts . . . thousand bags a week 'stead of fifty.

EFF EX: (*Tolerantly*): Joe, you don't understand the problem. If the volume of peanut sales increases our operating costs will go up . . . you'll have to handle more bags with more time, more depreciation, more everything. The basic principle of accounting is firm on that subject. 'The Bigger the Operation the More General Overhead Costs that must be Allocated'. No, increasing the volume of sales won't help.

JOE: Okay, You so smart, *you* tell *me* what I gotta do.

EFF EX (*Condescendingly*): Well . . . you could first reduce operating expenses.

JOE: How?

EFF EX: Move to a building with cheaper rent. Cut salaries. Wash the windows bi-weekly. Have the floor swept only on Thursday. Remove the soap from the washrooms. Decrease the square foot value of your counter. For example, if you can cut your expenses 50%, that will reduce the amount allocated to peanuts from $1,563 to $781.50 per year, reducing the cost to 36c per bag.

JOE (*Slowly*): That's better?

EFF EX: Much, much better. However, even then you would lose 26c per bag if you only charge 10c. Therefore, you must also raise your selling price. If you want a net profit of 4c per bag you would have to charge 40c.

JOE (*Flabbergasted*): You mean even after I cut operating costs 50% I still gotta charge 40c for a 10c bag of peanuts? Nobody's that nuts about nuts! Who'd buy 'em?.

EFF EX: That's a secondary consideration. The point is, at 40c you'd be selling at a price based upon a true and proper evaluation of your then reduced costs.

JOE (*Eagerly*): Look! I gotta better idea. Why don't I just throw the nuts out . . . put 'em in a ash can?

EFF EX: Can you afford it?

JOE: Sure. All I got is about 50 bags of peanuts . . . cost about three bucks . . . so I lose $25 on the rack, but I'm outa this nutsy business and no more grief.

EFF EX: (*Shaking head*): Joe, it isn't that simple. You are in the peanut business: The minute you throw those peanuts out you are adding $1,563 of annual overhead to the rest of your operation. Joe . . . be realistic . . . *can you afford to do that*?

JOE (*Completely crushed*): It's a unbelievable! Last week I was a make money. Now I'm in a trouble . . . just because I think peanuts on a counter is a gonna bring me some extra profit . . . just because I believe 50 bags of peanuts a week is a easy.

EFF EX (*With raised eyebrows*): That is the object of modern cost studies, Joe . . . to dispel those false illusions.

This last example illustrates the sort of arguments that so upset several engineers towards the end of the last century that they devoted their efforts to finding a more satisfactory approach. The result of this work provided the basis for cost-volume-profit analysis. It is perhaps salutary for accountants to remember that their profession created the problem but not the solution to overhead allocation.

Before considering alternative means of presenting information on costs of output, it is necessary to take an apparent diversion into one aspect of cost-volume-profit analysis: that of break-even analysis. The reason will be evident later.

10.2 THE BREAK-EVEN POINT

R. H. Parker[1] describes how the first article on break-even charts appeared in the American *Engineering Magazine* in December 1902. The article set out the manner in which costs behave — some remaining constant, and some varying in direct proportion to output — and the point at which total revenue exactly equalled total cost was defined as the break-even point, the point at which the firm made zero profit. At outputs above the break-even point the firm will make a profit as revenue exceeds cost, and below break-even output there will be a loss as revenue is less than cost.

Fig. 10.1

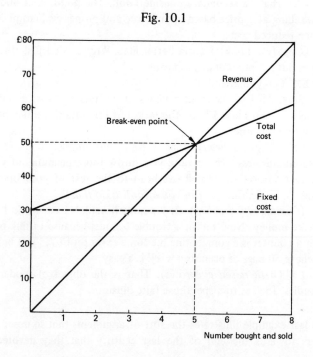

Number bought and sold

To illustrate a break-even chart, take the case of a man renting a stall in an antique market. The rent for the stall is £30 for the day of the market, and he has several framed prints which he has bought on sale or return from a supplier. These prints cost him £4 each and he is selling them for £10.

This information can be put into a break-even chart as illustrated in Fig. 10.1. This chart shows the total cost and revenue for various levels of sales, and there is a break-even point at five units of sale. At this point total cost exactly equals total revenue. The total cost is built up of two component parts: the fixed rental of £30 for the stall, which remains constant however many prints are sold; and the variable cost of £4 per print.

It is possible to produce a matrix of these data in the following form:

Number bought and sold	Fixed cost	Variable cost	Total cost	Revenue	Profit/ loss
0	£30	£0	£30	£0	£ -30
1	£30	£4	£34	£10	£−24
2	£30	£8	£38	£20	£−18
3	£30	£12	£42	£30	£−12
4	£30	£16	£46	£40	£−6
5	£30	£20	£50	£50	£−0
6	£30	£24	£54	£60	£+6
7	£30	£28	£58	£70	£+12
8	£30	£32	£62	£80	£+18

This matrix highlights the fact that if no prints are sold there will be a loss of £30. The rental for the stall will have to be paid whether or not there are any sales. The break-even point of five units is shown, together with the fact that if eight prints are sold, there will be a profit of £18.

The break-even chart can be redrawn to illustrate these facts (Fig. 10.2). This type of chart is called a profit/volume chart, and uses a single line to represent the three lines in the traditional break-even chart. It is possible to read off the profit or loss for any given volume of output and sale without having to measure the distance between the cost line and revenue line on the break-even chart.

To discover the break-even point there is a formula, whose solution is simpler than drawing break-even charts for each occasion. The break-even point is the level of output and sale at which total costs exactly equal total

Fig. 10.2

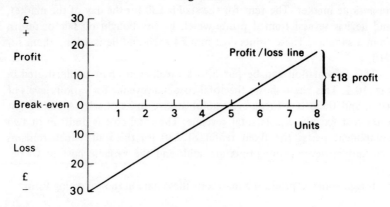

revenue. Profit is zero at this point.

Zero profit is where ⟶ Total cost = Total revenue

The two sides of this simple equation can be divided into their component parts:

Total revenue = Price multiplied by the number of units sold
Total cost = Fixed costs + (Variable cost multiplied by the number of units sold)

Thus, to find the break-even point it is necessary to find how many units have to be made and sold to complete the equation:

Price x Number of units
  ↓   ↓
  a   x

= Fixed cost + (Variable cost x Number of units)
       ↓   ↓   ↓
=   b   c   x

Giving each factor an algebraic symbol, the equation now becomes:

$$ax = b + cx$$

Solving this for x, the result is:

$$x = \frac{b}{a - c}$$

Converting this back into words, the number of units to be made and sold to provide zero profit is found by the following calculation:

$$= \frac{\text{Total fixed cost}}{\text{Unit price} - \text{Unit variable cost}}$$

To illustrate, the data on the stallholder can be used. The fixed costs were £30, the price was £10 and the variable cost £4.

$$\begin{array}{l}\text{Number of units to be bought} \\ \text{and sold to break even}\end{array} = \frac{£30}{£10 - £4} = 5 \text{ units}$$

10.3 PROBLEMS WITH BREAK-EVEN CHARTS

Why is the traditional break-even chart rarely used as a decision-making aid in real life? It is an ideal visual aid, and can be used at meetings, particularly sales and marketing meetings, to great effect. However, so many unrealistic assumptions are built into the three lines which appear on the chart that it is useless for management decision-making. These assumptions are:

(i) The costs associated with producing the various levels of output are constant, or at least capable of being approximated by straight lines.

(ii) Only one selling price — i.e. no discounts for large quantities or for most favoured customers — enabling revenue to be shown as a straight line.

(iii) A constant level of efficiency in production.

(iv) Fixed costs remain constant over the range of output considered.

(v) No significant changes in inventory levels.

(vi) Cost and revenue are only affected by volume changes.

(vii) Costs can accurately be estimated over all levels of output.

The examples so far have covered production and sale of only one product. If several products are made and sold, there is a further assumption which makes the break-even chart inoperable as a decision-making tool:

(viii) That there is a constant sales mix.

A variable discount structure can be shown in the sales revenue line, though it does complicate the chart. If the fixed costs change at a certain level of operations — perhaps more space has to be rented — this can give rise to a second break-even point. In the case of the stall-holder and the sale of prints, if he can hire an assistant and increase the size of his stall for £18, it will double his sales potential, but also produce a second break-even point, as can be seen from Fig. 10.3. There are two points at which total revenue equals total costs. Five units and eight units bought and sold produce zero profit. This information can provide a useful basis upon which to assess sales forecasts. If the stall-holder considers that he will sell about eight of the prints, then he does not need more space and assistance, and can look for a profit maximum of £18. If, however, he feels with the increased space and assistance he can push sales up to 16 units, then it will be worth going for a profit of £48. While the break-even chart has not provided solutions, it has pointed out key areas for further discussion and study. This is the best any chart can do.

Fig. 10.3

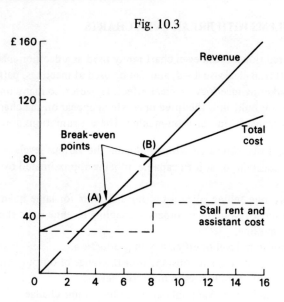

10.4 CONTRIBUTION ANALYSIS

If a break-even chart is no help in decision-making, how can the notion of break-even be used?

The formula for finding the break-even point is:

$$\frac{\text{Number of units for}}{\text{break-even}} = \frac{\text{Total fixed costs}}{\text{Unit price} - \text{Unit variable cost}}$$

Using the example from the beginning of this chapter, if the direct or variable unit costs (costs that vary in proportion to changes in volume of output) are set out, they appear as:

Materials	£5
Labour	4
Other	3
	£12 per unit

Given that the fixed costs are £7,000, it is a simple task using the break-even formula to calculate the number of units to be made and sold to break even:

$$\frac{£7,000}{£22 - £12} = 700 \text{ units}$$

The difference between unit price and unit direct or variable cost is £10. This £10 is termed the *unit contribution*. The first 700 units contribute £7,000 towards the recovery of the fixed costs of the firm. As the £12 direct costs have been recovered in arriving at the £10 contribution, this means that at 700 units the firm has a break-even point. If the firm makes and sells the 1,000 units shown in the budget for the year, then the remaining 300 units will provide £3,000 contribution to profit.

Such calculations provide an easy check that the correct break-even point has been found:

Break-even volume	700 units equals	zero profit
Balance left of budget	300 units at £10 per unit =	£3,000 profit
Budget sales	1,000 units with profit of	£3,000

If it is necessary to calculate the break-even point in terms of sales revenue, two methods can be adopted. The first is to take sales price over contribution and use this as a multiple on the fixed costs:

Price	£22
Variable costs	12
Contribution	10
	£22

$$\frac{\text{Price £22}}{\text{Contribution £10}} = 2.2$$

Fixed costs (£7,000) x 2.2 = £15,400
(700 units at a price of £22 = £15,400)

This shows a sales revenue of £15,400 for the break-even level.

The second method is to calculate the contribution percentage and use this rather than the unit contribution in the break-even formula. The contribution percentage in this case is:

$$\frac{\text{Contribution £10}}{\text{Price £22}} \times 100 = 45.45\%$$

Applying this in the break-even formula:

$$\frac{\text{Fixed costs £7,000}}{\text{Contribution percentage 0.4545}} = £15,400$$

Having discovered the break-even point, it is worth comparing the break-even volume with the sales budget. In this case 70 per cent of the sales budget must be achieved before the company begins to make a profit. This gives some indication of the 'margin of safety' of the product. If the break-even volume is considered too high a percentage of the sales budget – i.e. there is too small a margin of safety – then management may concentrate on trying to reduce the fixed costs or to change the direct costs or price.

With an understanding of break-even analysis and the concept of contribution, we can now move towards an assessment of marginal costing. In most situations:

Marginal costing = Direct costing = Variable costing

= Contribution analysis

Where companies separate their variable costs of output and sale from the fixed expenses, they are adopting some form of marginal costing. Faced with the information available the accountant has to assume that the marginal cost of a product is the same as the variable costs that can be set against that product. However, there will always be differences in the ways in which companies treat various types of cost. For example, in the current example labour has been treated as a completely variable cost, but a team of skilled employees may in effect be a fixed cost. They cannot be fired and hired as need indicates, but must be maintained in employment over long periods, as one of the company's real resources.

Marginal costing can conjure the image of declining prices, cut-throat competition and low profits, but it is very useful for providing quick pointers to decisions. It is also extensively used in export marketing. One marketing manager has described its application thus: 'When we use it on them it's good business; when they use it on us, it's dumping'.

Suppose the firm in our example has sold 800 units of the product for £22, and in the last few weeks of the year sees the market dry up. They are then offered £1,800 for 100 units. Had the firm been using full costing, the cost would have appeared as £19 per unit, and so the order would probably have been rejected. But what would the real impact on profitability be?

The unit contribution has now become £6 (price £18 less direct costs £12), and as the company has already passed the break-even point in sales, this £6 is a contribution to profit. Thus, selling 100 units at £18 will provide an additional £600 profit:

Profit on 800 units	£1,000	(£10 x 100 units)
Profit on 100 units	600	(£6 x 100 units)
Total profit	£1,600	

Indeed, as long as the product is sold above its marginal cost of £12, this will contribute to profit once the break-even volume has been reached.

This illustrates how marginal costing can be applied to export marketing. If the firm were able to sell 1000 units on the home market with a price of £22 to provide the required profit level of £3,000, and there were spare capacity available without incurring additional fixed costs, it might consider selling in another market overseas. As long as a price to the firm of over £12 were to be achieved, overall profit would be increased. The same product can be offered in separate markets at different prices and yet each market be profitable for the firm concerned. Where there is spare capacity available, marginal cost pricing is a useful method of providing extra income.

There are, of course, problems with such an application of marginal costing. If a firm were to sell its product at a marginal cost price at the end of the financial year just to increase profits for that year, it might find customer resistance when it tried to bring its price back to normal in the following year. The firm might encounter resistance from competitive producers (though probably not customers or distributors) in the export market. And there is always the possibility of the firm's existing customers seeking out the cheapest source, either themselves directly or via a third party. There have been cases where a firm has exported its product at low price, and then found that a keen-eyed businessman has brought these same products back to the home market to sell them at a lower price than the company charges. This activity is known as arbitrage. It is important that managers understand that even though a product may be returning a contribution, there is no guarantee that the total contribution will be sufficient to cover the fixed cost associated with that product, let alone provide a profit. A contribution does not mean an automatic profit. For example, if all 1,000 units of the product used in the examples so far had been sold at a price of £18, which provides a unit contribution of £6, the situation at the year end would have been:

Revenue 1,000 units at £18	= £18,000	
Direct costs	£12,000	*loss* £1,000
Indirect costs	£7,000	£19,000

At a price of £18 the break-even is 1,167 units, producing just over £21,000 revenue.

Contribution analysis can be of assistance in a pricing situation where the question is whether to reduce the price of a product. A frequent argument is that if the price is brought down, this will generate increased sales volume and greater profitability. But one must first discover how much increased volume is required to stand still, i.e. to make the same profit as under the existing price. This can be done as follows:

If the price of the product is reduced from £22 to £17 there will be increased sales and profitability for the firm. How many units must be sold before profitability is increased?

$$\text{Units} = \frac{\text{Fixed costs £7,000 + Planned profit £3,000}}{\text{Unit price £17} - \text{Unit variable cost £12}}$$

$$= \frac{£10,000}{£5}$$

$$= 2,000$$

Conclusion: To make the same profit as was planned with a price of £22 it will be necessary to produce and sell twice as much product.

The break-even formula has been used not to find the number of units that will produce zero profit, but the number which would generate the originally planned profit of £3,000. With this information, management can consider whether it is worth doubling production and sales for the same profit level. However, if they consider it possible to sell as much as 3,000 units, then the resulting profit of £8,000 may well prove attractive. But capacity must also be considered — perhaps fixed costs will be increased if greater production volumes are to be attained. If so, the volume needed to produce a £3,000 profit will be even greater.

Marginal costing and contribution analysis focus attention on those factors that are important and relevant to a decision. To illustrate this, consider the following financial statement on three products made and sold by a firm:

	A £'000	B £'000	C £'000	Total £'000
Sales revenue	900	600	300	1,800
Cost of goods sold:				
Variable	390	295	205	890
Fixed	150	100	50	300
Selling Expenses:				
Variable	80	60	70	210
Fixed	75	50	25	150
Total costs	695	505	350	1,550
Pre-tax profit/loss	205	95	(50)	250

From this report it would appear that product *C* is unprofitable and management could decide to drop it thereby increasing overall profit by £50,000. But is this really the case? Is this the right information upon which to base a decision? In both cases the answer is no. The proper way of presenting the financial information is as follows:

	A £'000	B £'000	C £'000	Total £'000
Sales revenue	900	600	300	1,800
Variable costs:				
Cost of goods sold	390	295	205	890
Selling expenses	80	60	70	210
Contribution	430	245	25	700
Fixed costs				450
Pre-tax profit				£250

Setting the information out in this format highlights the total contribution to fixed costs and eventual profit that each product generates, and provides the basis for a more satisfactory decision on product *C*.

In fact product *C* provides £25,000 contribution to fixed costs and profit. If this product is dropped and there is no reduction in total fixed costs, then the firm will make £25,000 less profit than at present. This is because the fixed costs will have to be absorbed by the two remaining products *A* and *B*. The £50,000 loss shown for *C* will go, but the £75,000 fixed costs it is bearing will remain.

The decision-makers can now focus on the basic question of how much fixed costs really relate to product *C*. In the original financial analysis, fixed costs were allocated in proportion to sales revenue (9:6:3), but it is most unlikely that this represents the true incidence of such costs. Allocating fixed costs on the basis of revenue in effect assumes that an increase in revenue (which could be brought about by a price increase) will automatically increase the fixed costs associated with that product. If different methods of allocation were used, a different spread of profit would be shown between the three products. Indeed, it is possible to make the profit appear under any one of the products, depending on the allocation method chosen. Using the contribution approach removes this difficulty, as the fixed costs are not allocated to individual products but merely shown as a deduction from the overall contribution.

If more than £25,000 of fixed costs will be eliminated if product *C* is dropped, then the firm will make more profit than if it kept this product. If less than £25,000 fixed costs will be lost, then the firm is better off keeping product *C*.

This type of analysis can also be applied to the assessment of divisional performance. It is not unusual to find reporting systems used to compare the profitability and general performance of divisions, yet with head office expenses allocated on some arbitrary basis between divisions. This obscures the real situation. Had the three products in the previous example been three divisions in a company and the fixed expenses been those of head office, the problem would have been the same. Division C appears to be less profitable than the other divisions. Such arbitrary allocations of fixed costs should be avoided. Management in divisions should only be judged on the costs and revenues that they can control or influence. If division C is making no use of head office services, it is better to judge it on the basis of a £25,000 contribution than a £50,000 loss.

A further discussion of control, analysis and assessment of performance is provided in Chapter 11.

10.5 CONTRIBUTION AND PRICING

In the previous section the use of marginal cost in export pricing was mentioned, but its use extends beyond the export situation.

Managers often argue that in order to set a price they must know the full cost of the product. This is frequently asserted where there is divisional responsibility for price-setting – that head office expenses should be allocated to divisions so the divisional manager knows what costs he must recover to make a 'profit'. This is a difficult point of view. It suggests that managers are incapable of getting the best price for their products except on a full costing basis. Certainly all costs must be recovered before a profit is made, but fixed costs should only have a limited impact on the pricing decision. The extreme conclusion to this logic would be a situation in which a head office with several divisions would allocate a much greater amount of 'fixed costs' to each division so as to ensure even higher profitability. Allocation of fixed costs may provide a psychological crutch to management in the pricing decision, but if they aim to maximise overall contribution from their products, they will automatically get the best profit. And this assessment of contribution must include consideration of how the market is likely to react to price changes — the 'price elasticity' of demand.

11 Budgeting, Budgetary Control and Corporate Planning

In the previous two chapters cost behaviour and costing systems were discussed. In this chapter budgeting and budgetary control are considered. The word 'budget' comes from the French for a small bag or purse, and came to be associated with the Chancellor of the Exchequer's bag, which contains his annual estimate of the country's income and expenditure in the national budget. The Chancellor is concerned with planning, co-ordinating and controlling income and expenditure for the government. The same tasks confront a manager in a firm.

A simple diagram of some aspects of the manager's job will illustrate the place of budgeting in the system (Fig. 11.1). It is a specific quantified plan over a period of time (normally one year) for the units of the organisation, against which performance may subsequently be assessed. Ideally, it helps to integrate and co-ordinate, and provides the basis for the financial planning discussed earlier in this book.

The budget documents embody the figures (quantification of plans, targets, measurement of actual outcomes), but it is clear from the diagram that they can achieve nothing without appropriate managerial activity.

In 1916 Henri Fayol[1] suggested that the management process consisted of planning, organisation, command, co-ordination and control. Planning involves deciding what is to be done (often from a large set of possible alternatives), and how it is to be carried out. Senior executives typically have the task of considering the overall objectives of the firm, and responsibility for setting the plan for their achievement, with detailed studies and co-ordination perhaps performed by a special corporate planning department. After consultation as to what is feasible, the functional manager will probably be given guidance as to what he should aim for in his area, but be left freedom as to method. Corporate planning and objectives are discussed in more detail in the next section.

Just as formulation of the plan logically follows upon consideration of company objectives, so organisation of human and physical resources

Fig. 11.1

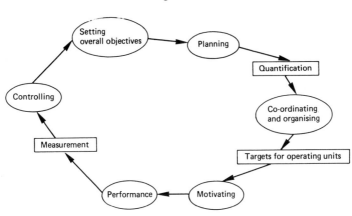

follows the plan. But the actual process of planning and budgeting is more complicated than our diagram shows, for formulation of policy must take account of the resources available, both human, physical and financial, and the firm's existing markets and investments, its strengths, weaknesses and opportunities. And except in periods of crisis or rapid expansion, the overall plan will contain a large chunk of continuing activity. So while the logical sequence appears clear, the actual process of planning and budgeting usually requires successive revision, compromise and focusing down, to arrive at the detail of a department's operating budget. And this budget requires both organisation (internal) and co-ordination (with other departments) of the human and physical resources. It used to be believed that plant and machinery required plugging into the power source, humans into the money source. Sometimes the latter form of motivation alone may work, but typically the matter of motivation is more complicated, depending both on the nature of the work and the individuals and groups involved, including the managers in charge. The behavioural side of budgeting is discussed below.

As the plan is implemented, the manager monitors performance and assesses how far it has gone towards achievement of its goals and whether any control action is necessary. Often it will be necessary to adjust plans in the light of operating experience or changes in the environment facing the firm. So when the plan is formulated, the objectives or targets must be quantified, and in organising and motivating, definite targets for performance should be set. The plan must be operational. The definition of a budget provided by the Institute of Cost and Management Accountants in an introductory text is: 'A financial and/or quantitative statement, prepared prior to a defined period of time, of policy to be pursued during that period for the purpose of attaining a given objective.' Though budgets are most commonly expressed in financial terms, there is no necessity for this. The budget should be set in terms meaningful to the organisation and its managers.

The first step in any budgeting activity is to recognise what it is that the firm is trying to achieve through its operations — its corporate objectives.

11.1 CORPORATE OBJECTIVES AND BUDGETING

Budgeting is concerned with planning, co-ordinating and controlling, but these activities presuppose an underlying objective. The plan, whether it is strategic or tactical, is concerned with the 'how', not with the 'what'. A plan or budget can usually be better formulated if the objectives are clearly defined. A simple view is that all that matters is profit, and that this is therefore the objective of the firm — indeed, the reason for its existence. For many years theoretical economists insisted that profit maximisation was the dominant objective of a business.

Unfortunately, the practical interpretation of this objective is not so simple. Not the least of the problems with the profit is the time-scale against which it is to be set. Over what period is the firm 'maximising' profit? It may be possible to make large profits today, but sacrifice longer term profitability, or even survival. Some shareholders may prefer this option, others not. Are all shareholders to be treated as if they had the same time- and risk-preferences? Suppose that management adopt a consistent policy in terms of risk and the firm's longer term future, leaving shareholders to show their preferences via the stock market, this still gives no guide as to what this policy should be.

These are problems of practical interpretation of the theoretical objective of profit maximisation. But the matter is further complicated. The last half-century has seen a trend away from owner-managed firms to widely held companies run by professional managers. How should share-holders' and managers' interests be reconciled? And how account for the interests of employees, whose employment and involvement is often far more than a simple exchange of labour in return for money? To say that profit maximisation (however interpreted) should be the dominant objective is to make a strong assertion about the appropriate distribution of power within a firm, and the exercise of such power calls forth reactions from the interested parties. The effect is a constraint on profits from increased wages and salaries, executive remuneration packages, welfare benefits and other overheads, and perhaps industrial action. So exclusive concentration on profit may well serve to limit profits. There are in addition interests beyond the firm – local communities, government, suppliers, customers – who may make their presence felt in boardroom and balance sheet. So the assertion of faith in profit maximisation does not help towards establishment of practical corporate objectives. What is required is a statement of longer term policy objectives which can guide the establishment of the shorter run operational planning targets. And the achievement of a more than satisfactory return on shareholders' equity should be part of this objective.

In the late 1950s and early 1960s several major American companies tackled this problem of formulating practical corporate objectives. One company which provided information on both its success and failure was General Electric. It developed a checklist of 'key areas' that any firm must consider in looking to the future. These key areas are:

   (i) market standing;
   (ii) innovation;
   (iii) productivity;
   (iv) profitability;
   (v) management development;
   (vi) employee attitudes;
   (vii) public responsibility;
   (viii) balance between short- and long-term activities.

The list does not rank the key areas – their relative importance varies according to the industry and firm. But all are important and all require consideration by management. If a firm fails in one of the key areas, it may put its entire operations in jeopardy.

Market standing can be assessed along various dimensions. The most simple is sales volume, and its growth pattern over time. But in a market growing 50 per cent a year, a company's sales can grow 25 per cent a year, showing apparently excellent growth, but lagging sadly behind competitors. Measurement of market share takes this key factor into account. More detailed consideration of the company's market standing will include consideration of its geographical penetration, its penetration in specialist segments of the market (by industry or customer taste or type), customer perception of its products and services, its pricing and promotional strategies, its profitability and distribution cost and coverage. This information about the company's standing must be set against data on competitors and considered in the light of the potential market. Is it mature, with sales coming from replacement or repeat purchases, or taking off? Will growth in sales have to come from competitors' customers, or from new customers? Careful assessment of data on these areas should enable a company to recognise and capitalise on its strengths and minimise its weaknesses. Few companies in few markets can be strong in all areas — there is always room for firms to carve out segments by specialising in such features as special design to customer order, local distribution and service, incorporation of new design features, and so on. The key task is to identify those areas of greatest market (and profit) potential which best suit the company's special strengths and abilities. This will then enable a practical operational plan to be formulated.

If the firm wishes to achieve or maintain some form of product leadership, this may require technical innovation resulting from research and development carried out by the firm. General Electric had a clear intention to be first in the field with new products and innovations on existing product lines. But even a firm with no such ambition must still consider its policy in this area. Is it merely going to match competition, or concentrate on some other form of product leadership, such as offering the best value for money to customers?

Productivity is also of vital importance to any organisation, since it affects its cost structure relative to the competition. A firm must assess how its productivity may be best measured, which are the key functions where productivity is important, and how this can be improved over time.

Profitability is a factor supposedly always given close attention by management. Profits are directly related to the previous key areas. Market share, which may be obtained through innovation, produces revenue, and productivity ensures efficient use of resources, lower costs, and improved profit levels.

Management and personnel development is also critical. There is little point in planning for growth if there are not going to be sufficient able managers. Recruitment may be able to supplement internal development, but all managers think in terms of their career paths and longer term development. If they do not see suitable prospects and opportunities ahead, they tend to leave — often the most able first. The humans in a firm may be its most important resources. It is the employees that enable the firm to be run effectively and to achieve its objectives. The way in which they view their work and its environment can have a direct impact on productivity and profitability. So the attitudes of managers and all personnel must be recognised and managed if they are to be deployed effectively and profitably.

General Electric was one of the first firms publicly to recognise the importance of public responsibility as a corporate objective. The company exists within a community. It not only provides continued employment, but also maintains the 'rules' of the community. Today, with the emphasis on avoiding pollution, this has even more relevance. The firm can no longer afford to ignore its environment, but has to accept its place and obligations in society. By regulating itself, it may pre-empt damaging and restrictive legislation aimed at achieving the same end.

The final key area in the list is especially important in companies with long lead-time capital investments. But every manager must always be careful that he does not unconsciously go for immediate apparently favourable results with an adverse impact in the longer term. For example, a firm can improve profitability by reducing the quality of its products while maintaining price. In the short term this may well be successful, but the longer term effect may be to alienate its customers, and gain a reputation for poor quality which is very expensive to counteract. Similarly customers can be loaded up with discounted stock this year, making current sales look good, but killing next year's sales. Equipment can be run on reduced maintenance, saving short-term costs, but at great long-term expense. Every decision and policy statement must be considered not only in the light of its current impact but also as to its longer term effects on the business as a whole.

All these key areas have a connection with the financial resources of the company. Executive management will have to consider how their plans are to be financed and the cash flow implications. Often finance will be the limiting factor, and therefore must be a separate but simultaneous key area for management consideration.

Examination of a key area may show that an area has no current applicability to the firm and can be discounted. However, the exercise of assessing the key area's importance is valuable in itself. The danger comes when management ignores a key area by default, not when this is done after careful assessment.

Where key areas are relevant, objectives should be framed in clear terms. The objectives should have the following features if they are to be of practical use. They should:

  (i) act as a guide to specific action by those concerned;
 (ii) be capable of measurement;
(iii) be ambitious enough to challenge;
 (iv) take account of internal and external constraints;
  (v) be related to the higher and lower objectives in that area.

In formulating policy, it is helpful to consider such questions as 'What business are we really in?'; 'Where do we want to be as a firm in five years' time?; and 'How do we get there?'. The answers must accommodate the external and internal constraints and the strengths and weaknesses of the firm.

If undertaken seriously, this corporate planning process becomes a focus of conflict. Such conflict is inevitable where there is competition between divisions for valued resources such as capital for preferred projects, additional staff, promotional budgets, and so on. Furthermore, in most firms there exists potential for conflict between departments, where there is interdependence with different values. The sales manager may look for large discounts, many options and immediate delivery, for his concern is usually to increase sales volume and satisfy customers. But often this can only be achieved by disrupting production schedules, and reducing profit margins, when every favoured customer becomes a case for special treatment. Conversely, the production manager will favour few products, larger volumes and longer runs, but above all, stability for his production planning. Other managers will be looking for other factors which compound these conflicts. The challenge to senior managers then is to find constructive ways of channelling such conflict, of providing co-ordination between differing departmental requirements, and integration of differing values. In this, senior managers play the role of politicians, weighing up conflicting claims, ambitions and perspectives, engineering compromise and balance between alternative views, without compromising the firm's overall objectives. In this context a clearly stated and widely accepted corporate policy can help to integrate and reconcile such conflicting values and interests.

The clearer a company's product-market stance, and the more specialised its activities, the easier it is to have a simple, clearly stated corporate objective. However, where firms consist of conglomerations of unrelated companies, it is hard to provide an operational all-embracing policy, except in performance terms such as market leadership, growth rates and return on capital. In such cases it is probably best to concentrate on providing objectives for related groups or units. A compromise form of words which conceals real differences of view is not likely to provide a clear guide to action. As always, it is not the technique of corporate planning and budgeting, but the processes by which policy is hammered out, resources allocated, and compromises and agreements reached, which is important. Planning and budgeting can serve to assist in this process of co-ordinating activities, and integrating values towards a common end. The less the disagreement on this common end, the more the firm is likely to make a success of its corporate planning.

11.2 BUDGETARY CONTROL

Budgetary control is a system where budgets are prepared for the various activities of a firm, and actual performance is regularly compared with budget. To be fully effective, the budgetary control system must be devised with close attention to organisational structure. The budgets should be consistent with the responsibility centres of the firm. A budget for a manager should consist of explicit recognition of the resources at his disposal, how they are to be used during the budget period, and what is expected to be the end result of their deployment. Budgets are normally expressed in financial terms and all the individual responsibility centres brought together in a Master Budget which is a Profit and Loss Statement and Balance Sheet for the end of the budget period. However, individual managers may have their own sections of the overall budget put into terms which are relevant to their responsibilities, leaving the accountant to translate these into financial terms when necessary.

Given the overall objectives of the firm, and the strategy for meeting them, the next stage is to prepare a series of statements which set out the key responsibility areas' intended actions for the budgeting period. These individual budgets are interrelated and in total offer a budget Profit and Loss Account and Balance Sheet, as illustrated in Fig. 11.2.

Fig. 11.2

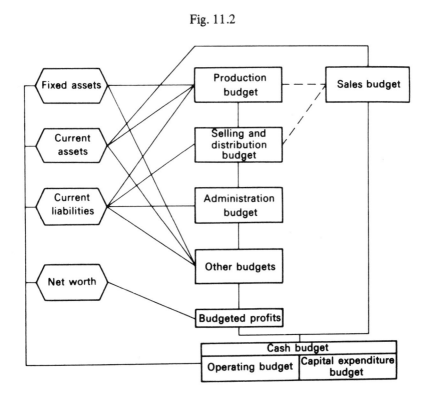

Where should the budgeting process start? Often the logical starting point is with sales. Sales tend to be the limiting factor for most firms since there are limits as to how much product can be sold or how much service can be offered. There is no reason why this should always apply, but a firm should start with the factor which limits its operations. Sometimes this may be productive capacity which should then be the starting point for the budgeting process.

Where sales are the limiting factor, the managers responsible for selling the products or services should prepare a sales forecast for the coming period: what they are going to sell, when and where it is to be sold, and who is going to sell it. It is best to consider first only unit sales, as these figures must be checked against productive capacity. Once the physical requirements of sales have been agreed with production they can be put into financial terms. The proposed prices are multiplied by the volume of sales to arrive at revenue for the period, and the costs of selling and distribution circulated.

In preparing a sales forecast, the manager must have some idea of the potential market for the products he is selling. This will involve a knowledge of who the firm's customers are, what competition there is or will be, and how price will affect demand. Often forecasts combine both the sales manager's judgement and the estimates of the marketing research department. An important concept from economic theory in this area is price elasticity — how volume will change as the price is increased or reduced. Estimating the sensitivity of the demand to price is essential in sales forecasting. If this knowledge is used in conjunction with the concepts of break-even analysis and contribution set out in Chapter 10, then sales revenue and profit can be more finely judged and budgeted.

The sales forecast and budget will depend on many external social, political and economic factors over which the firm has little control. Assumptions relating to forecasts should be made explicit in the budget, and discussed and agreed, since an assumption made in preparing the sales forecast will affect the production budget and the selling and distribution budgets, and all budgets which depend on the level of activity in the firm.

The production budget will be based upon the requirements for fulfilling the sales budget and will include not only production capacity but also changes in inventory levels of stock and finished goods. It should also include purchasing needs and labour requirements. Any capital investment necessary must also be budgeted. Finally these figures are quantified into a production cost budget which can be set against the sales revenue budget.

The following list summarises the information required for, and contained in, the sales and production budgets. These two form the lock into which other sub-budgets are keyed.

Sales Budget	*Production Budget*
Initial data requirements:	*Initial data requirements:*
Products to be sold, by area	Productive capacity
Sales force available	Inventory − materials
Type of customer segments	− work-in-progress
Assumptions about competitive	− finished goods
activities	Labour force available
Assumptions about environmental	Physical sales requirements
factors	− timing
	− types of product
Producing the budget:	*Producing the budget:*
Sales forecast	Sales forecast budget
− timing	− timing
− quantity	− nature of product
− customers	− quantity and mix
− areas	Materials purchasing budget
Marketing plan	Direct labour budget
Advertising and promotion plan	Overhead budget
Selling and distribution plan	Capital investment budget

Sales Budget   Inventory Budget   Production Budget

These budgets are quantified in financial terms by the accountant to bring in such factors as cash flow, credit policy, discount structure and price, together with delivery lead times, variation in stock levels and credit taken from suppliers. At this stage gross profit levels can be seen, and adjustments can be made before finalisation of the budgets. However, it is not only profits, revenues and costs that management is considering in this exercise, but also the cash flow. Cash budgeting is as critical as profit planning, and the cash budget derives from the various other budgets. There is little point in finalising a set of budgets if financial constraints make them impossible, so before budgets are worked out in detail, rough figures are usually provided in order to test for the constraints. Managers present their own budgets in terms meaningful to them; the accountant translates them into financial terms, and brings them all together in a profit statement and a cash budget.

The other areas for which budgets are prepared, such as administration, research and development, and general expenses, follow a similar pattern. For example, the personnel and training manager will develop a budget which reflects the requirements of both the sales and production budgets.

Employees will be recruited and trained to fulfil the firm's needs, and there will be a continuing set of expenses to maintain the personnel function in operation. All these will be budgeted and put into financial terms by the accountant for incorporation into both the profit statement and the cash budget.

11.3 ADMINISTRATION OF A BUDGETARY CONTROL SYSTEM

The mechanical side of budgets has been considered so far, and their co-ordinating and forecasting functions. But a significant part of budgetary control is concerned with the initiation of budgets, their agreement by senior executives, and their implementation by the managers concerned.

For effective budgetary control the responsible managers should participate in the setting of the budgets that relate to their responsibilities and activities. Otherwise the budgets may be either disregarded as unrealistic, or resented as an arbitrarily imposed target. The various functional managers usually draft their budget proposals for the coming period, but the manner in which this is compiled will vary from firm to firm. As an example, with a sales budget the steps might be as follows:

   (i)   Collect all available historic information on sales:
          − by product,
          − by area,
          − by customer,
          − by period.
   (ii)   Ensure full appreciation of the planned objectives of the firm as they affect sales in particular markets.
   (iii) Ask area/product sales managers for their assessment of the coming period's sales potential in the same classifications as in (i) above.
   (iv) Bring this information together and assess its implications for profit and for production requirements.
   (v)   Meet with senior sales managers to discuss (iv).
   (vi) Agree and set sales budgets for the various managers' responsibility areas.

Throughout this process the accountant will be presenting the possible sales strategies and policies in financial terms both for cash flow and profitability. If new products are planned, their launch will be programmed into the sales budget as well as the cash flow forecast.

Once the sales manager is satisfied with his budget he will present it to executive management, or the other managers in the firm, for discussion and eventual agreement. The sales budget will be set in the context of the other budgets and related to overall profitability and cash availability. For each budget area the manager concerned should present both his assumptions and planned actions, and once agreed the budget then becomes the main guide to the manager's activities for the coming period.

As with standard costing, a decision must be taken as to the level of attainment. Is it to be based on previous years' experience, probably providing an easy level of attainment for the manager; is an ideal level to be set that can only be achieved with perfect conditions and maximum efficiency; or is a level set that is possible, but which will require considerable effort? The problems of budgets and motivation are considered later in this chapter.

11.4 REPORTING UNDER BUDGETARY CONTROL

If a system of budgeting is to be of value there must be commitment from the senior executives. The budgeting system by itself will not guarantee better results or better control. While some benefit can be obtained just from the exercise of producing budgets, real benefits can only be obtained by their effective implementation.

At regular intervals, at least monthly, managers should compare their actual performance against budget, and analyse the causes for variances. It is helpful to show such variances from budget not only in financial or other quantified terms, but also as percentages, as illustrated in Fig. 11.3. A sales manager armed with this information has a useful tool. The current month's activity is set out, as well as figures for the year to date, and what must still be achieved if the year end results are to match those budgeted.

In reporting under budgetary control systems it is helpful to split the reports into two sections: the first dealing with those factors over which the manager has some direct control, and the second dealing with the various non-controllable factors such as rates, insurance, depreciation, etc.

What level of variance is significant and worthy of investigation? Budgetary control allows management by exception, where attention is focused on those areas which have not turned out as planned. If every variance is investigated, the system will grind to a halt or be disregarded. A level of ±10 per cent may be set as being the minimum level of variance worth investigation, but obviously it will depend on which section of operations is under assessment and the pattern and extent of fluctuations normally expected. It is possible to use simple statistical techniques to provide control limits for variances. By this means it would be possible to calculate to a conventional confidence level (99.8 or 95 per cent) the bounds within which results would be expected to fall. Where actual results fall beyond this, investigation is undertaken. This sort of analysis is particularly effective for repetitive production activities.

Fig. 11.3

	This month				Year to date				To year-end		
	Budget	Actual	+/−	%	Budget	Actual	+/−	%	Budget	Actual	Remaining
Units											
Product A	100	110	10	10	800	900	100	13	1,000	900	100
B	100	90	(10)	(10)	900	1,000	100	11	1,000	1,000	–
C	100	80	(20)	(20)	700	600	(100)	(14)	900	600	600
.											
.											
.											
Revenue (£)											
Product A	1,000	1,060	60	6	8,000	9,100	1,100	14	12,000	9,100	2,900
B	1,000	840	(160)	(16)	7,000	8,200	800	11	10,000	8,200	1,800
C	1,000	700	(300)	(30)	9,000	8,700	(300)	(3)	12,000	8,700	3,300

181

Graphical presentation of budget and actual performance data can provide a quick and easy means of identifying problem areas for further investigation. For example, the graph illustrated in Fig. 11.4 shows current year's sales revenue expressed as a percentage change from the budgeted sales for the year. This allows a much quicker appreciation of deviations from budget than a series of tables, and could be maintained as a wall chart in the manager's office and up-dated regularly.

Fig. 11.4

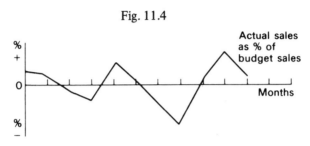

Fig. 11.5 shows selling and distribution expenses as a percentage of sales revenue, and allows speedy isolation of changes which require explanation.

Fig. 11.5

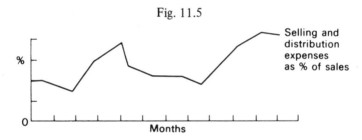

The same graphical approach can be used to monitor current assets by comparing actual levels with those budgeted, as set out in Fig. 11.6. With

Fig. 11.6

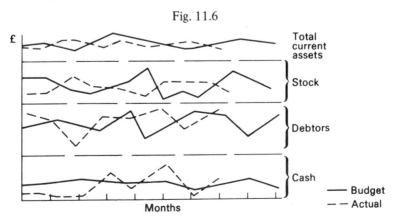

this graph the budgeted levels for cash, debtors and stock are compared with actual levels. This does not present different information from that contained in a typical budget report, but it does set it out in a manner that can be quickly appreciated and followed.

Finally, graphs can be used to show moving annual totals and cumulative differences. A moving annual total (MAT) is found by taking the previous eleven months' results and adding the current month's, then dividing by twelve. This is done each month, and if the changes between the MATs are studied this can show a trend developing in the area to which it is applied. If put into graphical form, the results are simple to follow. A cumulative difference is illustrated in Fig. 11.7. The graph shows the cumulative difference between actual and budgeted performance. As each month shows a difference this is added to the difference for the year to date, and plotted on the graph. This again allows quick awareness of changes or trends developing in the area graphed which call for attention and action. If the cumulative difference line continues to move away from the zero difference line this can indicate a trend that should be investigated. It is also possible to introduce control limit lines into this graph to indicate with greater precision the development of a trend.

Fig. 11.7

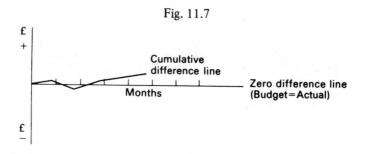

No manager should feel constrained by the traditional reporting system in operation in his firm. Graphical presentation is quick and simple to prepare, requiring no more information than the ordinary accounting/budgeting reports, and with graphs managers can see better what is happening in their area of responsibility.

11.5 FLEXIBLE BUDGETING

Where budgets are based on an estimated volume of output, and that volume is under- or overachieved, how are actual results compared with the budget? Under a system of flexible budgeting, costs and revenues are analysed to show how they react to volume changes. If the actual volume changes from budget, the actual performance figures are compared with the budget figures that relate to the volumes achieved during the period. An example of this is provided below:

	Budget at different volumes 1,000 hours	1,100	1,200	1,300	
Indirect labour	700	700	750	800	800
Maintenance	100	100	120	130	150
Power	100	110	120	130	140
Depreciation, etc	100	100	100	100	100
	£1,000	£1,010	£1,090	£1,160	£1,190

If 1200 hours work produces actual costs of £1,160, and the basis of comparison is a static budget level of £1,000 and 1,000 hours (£1 per hour worked), then there will be a favourable variance of £40:

1,200 hours worked at £1 per hour	£1,200
Actual cost incurred	£1,160
	£40

However, if the actual cost is compared with the flexible budget at 1,200 hours of work, then an adverse variance of £70 is shown:

Flexible budget figure for 1,200 hours	£1,090
Actual costs at 1,200 hours worked	£1,160
	−£70

The point here is that some costs do not vary directly with hours worked, and the flexible budget recognises this fact.

11.6 BEHAVIOURAL PROBLEMS WITH BUDGETARY CONTROL

In a 1952 study on 'The Impact of Budgets on People', Argyris[2] identified at least four possible human relations problems directly deriving from the use of budgets:

(i) Budget pressure tends to unite employees against management, and place the factory supervisor under tension, a tension which may lead to inefficiency, aggression and perhaps a complete breakdown.

(ii) Financial staff can obtain feelings of success only by finding fault with factory people, leading to feelings of failure among factory supervisors.

(iii) The use of budgets as 'needlers' by top management tends to make the factory supervisors see only the problems of their own departments. They are not concerned with other people's problems, and not 'plant-centred' in outlook.

(iv) Supervisors use budgets as a way of expressing their own patterns of leadership. When these patterns result in people getting hurt, the budget, in itself a neutral thing, often gets blamed.

The point to note here is that budgets are used for different purposes:

(i) Co-ordinating and integrating activities, an outcome of which is the planning of the cash budget.

(ii) Setting performance targets, motivating and controlling.

(iii) A plan of campaign, against which actual outcomes can be compared, providing clues as to where assumptions and forecasts may be off-target or mistaken. In this role budgets are used as part of a feedback mechanism in a communication system.

Argyris' findings seem to derive from cases where budgets have been used for the second purpose. Such faults are compounded when the budgeting system is tied to a bonus system, since this introduces an incentive for managers to beat the budget. The focus of activity then turns on the setting of the budget targets. Managers try to weight their budgets to ensure leeway, so that they can at least meet their budget. Limits are set on current performance, lest outstanding results this year get built into next year's norm. Enterprise and originality are devoted to devising a stable achievable set of indicators, rather than achieving the maximum possible in the context of market potential, human potential and availability of resources.

The dilemma is neatly summarised by the formula:

$$\text{Trust} + \text{Control} = \text{A Constant Sum}$$

Control cannot be increased without decreasing the degree of trust, and vice versa. With a decrease in trust, one gets a decrease in participation, possibly in concern for the firm's overall objectives. So one of the important questions to be answered in any budgeting system is how far the company's operations can be disaggregated for purposes of performance measurement. If there is a premium on co-operation and co-ordination between interdependent units attempts to split them up into responsibility

185

centres for the sake of control may well prove counterproductive. In going for its own budget targets, a department may fail to help, or even inhibit others meeting theirs. This is why the budgeting system should follow the appropriate organisational structure.

This question relates to the nature of the firm's operations, and the ways in which they can reasonably be split into components. But a further question concerns human motivation. In 1971 E. H. Caplan[3] reported the state of research in this area. There were deep conflicts between the (unstated) assumptions accountants were making in the traditional accounting control system in a firm, and the theories and observations of behavioural scientists. These assumptions covered three areas:

    (i)   organisational objectives;
    (ii) human behaviour;
    (iii) the management accounting system.

In a traditional system accountants tended to assume that the chief objective was to maximise profit, with a consensus on both ends and means. The problems with profit maximisation have been discussed in Section 11.1, and there is often also disagreement over objectives and ways of meeting objectives. Firms are structured groupings of individuals with personal ambitions and objectives, and different ways of formulating and viewing problems. The manner in which these individuals and groupings react and interact is vital to the firm's direction. In few companies of any size can a policy be imposed successfully from the top downwards. Furthermore the balance of the controlling group may change over time, leading to changes in the overall objectives of the firm. In a changing environment and a changing firm, policy objectives are not immutable. In the simple diagram at the beginning of this chapter (Fig. 11.1), allowance is made for objectives to be changed in the light of experience.

The second set of assumptions were caricatured by McGregor[4] as Theory X. The assumptions are that the average man is lazy by nature, and works as little as possible, lacking ambition and preferring to be led. He is inherently self-centred, resistant to change, and unconcerned with the organisation's objectives. Consequently managers (who are presumed not to be average men) have to do the organising, in the interest of economic ends, directing, motivating and controlling employees with money as an incentive, and with appropriate punishments and controls. Employees have to be treated with distrust. Two points are worth making. Even where employees seem to exhibit such characteristics, this may be a result of basic differences in values and objectives, not human nature. Second, a control and reward system which assumes such behaviour tends to elicit and reinforce such behaviour, thus confirming its own assumptions.

186

Within this second set of assumptions, the management accounting system was seen as mainly trying to assist management (or shareholders) to maximise profits, identify poor performance, and allocate targets with accurate information and a neutral approach. But it is clear that the way the system is used is by no means neutral. Furthermore, the budgeting system itself is not necessarily neutral and unambiguous, since accountants have wide discretion in how they present and interpret information, and are themselves part of the firm's political constituency, with their own personal and departmental concerns.

As a technique, budgetary control is relatively straightforward, but its application requires diagnosis of the firm's operating systems, and an understanding of the attitudes and behaviour of the groups involved. Since such information is particular to the firm and requires detailed insight and judgement, standardised prescriptions are not available. However, some tentative guidelines have been suggested by C. H. Handy[5] :

  (i)   An individual needs knowledge of both goals and results achieved if he is going to put extra effort into achievement (loose budgets are poor motivators).
 (ii)   Most individuals can be encouraged to set their targets higher by demonstrations that others have higher expectations of them.
(iii)   Different levels of targets will be effective for different individuals, depending on the implicit 'psychological contract' they have in working, and upon their sets of needs and perceptions of the rewards, psychological and other, for meeting those targets.
 (iv)   Targets for aspiration should be separated from budgets for planning.
  (v)   Budgets for planning cannot always be used in the continuing operations of the firm since the degree of accuracy and risk permitted or required will vary with the purpose of the budget.
 (vi)   Performance figures used as feedback against planning targets should be separated from figures for control. Budgets for control are only useful if they lead to corrective action from the responsible executive.

11.7 PPBS AND ZERO-BASE BUDGETING

In the 1960s the US Department of Defense introduced a system which came to be known as 'Planning, programming, budgeting systems' (PPBS or programme budgeting). The intention was to compare the outputs of programmes (how well they are achieving their declared objectives), and thus relate cost to effectiveness, looking ahead over the life of programmes, and comparing all policies related to common objectives. It has been widely tried in government agencies all over the world. But there is some doubt about its efficacy. Wildavsky[6] bluntly states that 'it does not work anywhere in the world it has been tried', partly because the requirements of relating causes to consequences in all important areas of policy are beyond individual or collective human capacity. It may be argued that this is a criticism of an overoptimistic view of PPBS, by which all possible programmes are compared. But Wildavsky argues further that PPBS increases the cost of correcting error in a fallible and changing world, that PPBS does not provide information relevant to the user at any level, whereas the traditional line-item budgeting system (with categories of personnel, maintenance, supplies) is easier to change. 'Budgeting by programmes, precisely because money flows to objectives, makes it difficult to abandon objectives without abandoning simultaneously the organisation that gets its money for them.' However, this is not to say that analysis should not take place at the level of policies and programmes, or that objectives, costs and benefits should not be considered. The fault with PPBS, according to Wildavsky, is that a temporary analytic insight is made the permanent perspective through which money is funnelled. One might add that there are two additional dangers from the application of any set of techniques. First, important questions and problems can be obscured or ignored by focusing attention on the application of a technique. Second, those who are expert in the technique thereby acquire power which may be used to divert or constrain the real contributions of the functional operating units.

PPBS was introduced as a way of assessing the outputs of organisations which traditionally had been controlled on the input side (cost-budgets). Most firms, whether private or public, have some degree of feedback from markets as to their performance, so that they cannot long survive without some attention to ends and objectives. But even in the private sector there is a continuing need to assess the budget bases. In the late 1960s and early 1970s Texas Instruments developed a system called 'zero-base budgeting'. This was developed from a need to reduce overall budgets in a particular year, when managers were asked what they would cut in order to meet the reduced budget level in that year. It was then considered worthwhile to discover exactly what the various units in the firm were going to do during the year. From this there arose a system by which each year management is required to produce a minimum level of activity budget for their operations that would cover the absolute minimum requirements to maintain an acceptable operating level, and then on top of this to prepare a series of 'decision packages' for levels above this. These decision packages show how additional funds would be used if they were available, and what the end return would be from each package. The packages are ranked in order of importance for the department or division, thus enabling manage-

188

ment to assess what will be produced if extra funds are allotted, and to make an objective allocation to departments of available resources beyond the minimum requirements. This system forces managers to re-evaluate all expenditures each year, and to justify their budget on the basis of what will be returned to the firm if they receive it. Note that this applies best in a divisionalised system where divisions have separate markets, rather than in a firm where departments are linked together in a sequential manner in a common endeavour to serve a single set of markets. But it is always worth asking what can be pruned, at what short- or long-term cost.

11.8 CONCLUSION

'If we can get accounting and human nature to work together, we have got something, but if they are opposing, we haven't solved the problem' (Rep. Wilfred McNeil, Committee on Government Operations, US House of Representatives, 1956).

Appendix 1 Acronyms

One of the more unfortunate aspects of modern accounting life is the ever increasing number of initials, abbreviations, and other shorthand that litter the literature. This Appendix attempts to provide a guide to the more common acronyms of the accounting scene.

ACA — Associate Member of the Institute of Chartered Accountants
ACAS — Advisory Conciliation and Arbitration Service
ACCA — Member of the Association of Certified Accountants
ACMA — Associate Member of the Institute of Cost and Management Accountants
ACT — Advance Corporation Tax
AISG — Accountants International Study Group
APC — Auditing Practices Committee
ASB — Auditing Statements Board
ASSC — Accounting Standards Steering Committee
CCA — Current Cost Accounting
CCAB — Consultative Committee of Accounting Bodies
CCOP
(or COP)— Current Cost Operating Profit
CGT — Capital Gains Tax
CIPFA — Chartered Institute of Public Finance and Accountancy
CLCB — Committee of London Clearing Bankers
COGS — Cost of Goods Sold
COSA — Cost of Sales Adjustment
CPE — Continuing Professional Education
CPP — Current Purchasing Power
CTT — Capital Transfer Tax
DCF — Discounted Cash Flow
DLT — Development Land Tax
DTI — Department of Trade and Industry

EBIT	–	Earnings Before Interest and Tax
ECI	–	Equity Capital For Industry Ltd
ED	–	Estate Duty
ED	–	Exposure Draft
EDITH	–	Estates Duty Investment Trust
EPS	–	Earnings per Share
FASB	–	Financial Accounting Standards Board (USA)
FCA	–	Fellow of the Institute of Chartered Accountants
FFI	–	Finance Corporation for Industry Ltd
FIFO	–	First in First Out
HAA	–	Human Asset Accounting
HCA	–	Historic Cost Accounting
IAG	–	International Auditing Guideline
IAPC	–	International Auditing Practices Committee
IASC	–	International Accounting Standards Committee
IASG	–	Inflation Accounting Steering Group
ICA	–	Institute of Chartered Accountants, or
ICAEW	–	Institute of Chartered Accountants in England and Wales
ICFC	–	Industrial and Commercial Finance Corporation
ICMA	–	Institute of Cost and Management Accountants
IED	–	International Exposure Draft
IFA	–	International Federation of Accountants
IRR	–	Internal Rate of Return
LIFO	–	Last in First Out
MLR	–	Minimum Lending Rate
MWCA	–	Monetary Working Capital Adjustment
NPV	–	Net Present Value
NRC	–	Net Replacement Cost
NRV	–	Net Realisable Value
OTC	–	Over the Counter Market (USA)
PAS	–	Practice Advisory Service
P/E	–	Price/Earnings Ratio
PPBS	–	Planning, Programming, Budgeting Systems
PSC	–	Professional Standards Committee
RC	–	Replacement Cost
RI	–	Residual Income
ROCE	–	Return on Capital Employed
ROI	–	Return on Investment
RONA	–	Return on Net Assets
RPI	–	Retail Price Index
SE	–	Stock Exchange
SEC	–	Securities Exchange Commission (USA)
SSAP	–	Statement of Standard Accounting Practice

UEC	— Union Européenne des Experts Comptables Economiques et Financiers
VA	— Value Added
VAT	— Value Added Tax
ZBB	— Zero-based Budgeting

Appendix 2 Value Added Statements

The *Corporate Report* in 1975 suggested that:

> There is evidence that the meaning and significance of profits are widely misunderstood. (6.8)

and

> The simplest and most immediate way of putting profit into proper perspective vis-á-vis the whole enterprise as a collective effort by capital, management and employees is by presentation of a statement of value added (that is, sales income less materials and services purchased). (6.7)

It also recommended that companies should consider the inclusion of value added as part of their reporting activities. The Pilkington 1979 Statement is illustrated here (Fig. A2.1). The Corporate Report (6.9) also recommended that the value added statement (VA) should include information on:

   (i)   Turnover (Pilkington £548.8m);
  (ii)   Bought-in materials and services (£259.1m);
 (iii)   Employees' wages and benefits (£167.7m + £27.2m);
 (iv)   Dividends and interest payable (£9.8m + £0.6m + £6.2m);
  (v)   Tax payable (£42.7m);
 (vi)   Amount retained for reinvestment (£44.3m + £35.9m + £1.3m);

and provided an example of the type of presentation that might be adopted (6.10). The statement in Pilkington Brothers Ltd 1979 Annual Report follows the pattern set out in the *Corporate Report*. Many major UK companies now provide such VA Statements in their Annual Reports. The Government Green Paper on 'The Future of Company Reports' reinforced the benefits of VA reporting (Dept. of Trade, Cmnd 6888, HMSO, 1977).

192

Group value added and its distribution

Value added is the wealth created by the group. This
statement shows how this wealth has been distributed
and the amount reinvested for use in the business.

		1979 £m		1978 £m
Sales to outside customers		548.8		469.5
Purchases of materials, fuel and services		259.1		220.3
Value added by trading operations		289.7		249.2
Licensing income		37.9		32.8
Income from associates and other investments		8.1		6.2
Total to be distributed		335.7		288.2
	%		%	
Distribution				
Payroll	58	194.9	58	167.2
wages and salaries		167.7		145.3
pension, social security and redundancy costs		27.2		21.9
Interest on borrowed money (net)	2	6.2	3	9.9
Dividends				
to Pilkington shareholders	3	9.8	3	7.2
to minority shareholders		.6		.3
Taxation	13	42.7	13	36.3
Reinvested in the business	24	81.5	23	67.3
amounts set aside for depreciation, replacement and obsolescence of buildings, plant and equipment		44.3		39.4
profit reinvested by Pilkington shareholders		35.9		26.9
profit reinvested by minority shareholders in subsidiaries		1.3		1.0
Total distribution of value added and other income	100	335.7	100	288.2

The above percentages are calculated on the 'Total
to be distributed,' which includes licensing
income as well as value added by trading
operations

	£	£
Group key ratios – average per employee		
Sales to outside customers	15,910	14,400
Value added by trading operations	8,400	7,640
Payroll costs	5,650	5,130
wages and salaries paid to employees	4,860	4,450
Reinvested in the business	2,360	2,060
depreciation etc. of buildings, plant and equipment	1,280	1,210

A VA Statement shows the wealth created by the company through its various operations, and how this has been distributed. The value added represents the total wealth created during the year by all interested parties:

(i)   Shareholders;
(ii) Directors and management;
(iii) Workforce;
(iv) Other providers of capital;

and the VA Statement balances the wealth created with its use during the year. All the information derives from the conventional annual accounts. From the VA Statement one can see what changes have occurred in the VA of a company, and how the shares of VA for the different interests have changed over time. Pilkington Brothers present percentage figures on VA to assist this process. For example payroll costs remained constant at 58 per cent of VA between 1978 and 1979; whereas the amount reinvested in the business rose from 23 to 24 per cent (Fig. A2.1).

Many companies have found VA Statements an effective means of communicating otherwise quite complex financial information to their employees. For example, the 1979 'Special Report' of Marks and Spencer Ltd, reproduced as Fig. A2.2, shows their staff 'How they Add Up. . . '. This combines VA information with financial data relating to the customers' pounds spent in a store. It shows that the 'profit' of the company for 1979 is divided between the providers of capital (£34.0m), the government in taxation (£76.2m), and reinvestment (£62.8m). In terms of pence per pound taken this works out at 2p, 5p and 5p respectively.

Simple ratios serve to highlight movements in VA. For example, Pilkington Brothers provide ratios developed on the basis of sales, VA, payroll, and reinvestment per employee for 1978 and 1979. Such Value Added Statements provide a simple and effective means of presenting complex financial information and will surely continue to be developed as part of the financial communication system adopted by companies.

Fig. A2.2

HOW THEY ADD UP...

HOW WE DID IN THE U.K.

		1978 - 79	1977 - 78
GOODS		£989.5m	£831.3m
VAT		£71.1m	£58.8m
PAY AND BENEFITS		£142.7m	£125.5m
RUNNING COSTS		£55.4m	£47.3m
PROFIT	TAX ON PROFIT	£76.2m	£53.9m
	DIVIDENDS	£34.0m	£27.6m
	DEVELOPMENT *	£62.8m	£49.0m
TOTAL		£1431.7m	£1193.4m

*Including depreciation, £11.9m this year, set aside to replace old equipment.

It's perhaps difficult to see figures in perspective when we talk in millions. So let's scale it down to terms of a pound. (We've used the new £1 gift token for our example).

Marks & Spencer Gift Voucher

St Michael

Value One Pound

This voucher can only be exchanged at Marks and Spencer stores in the United Kingdom

GOODS 69p

VAT 5p

PAY AND BENEFITS 10p

RUNNING COSTS 4p

TAX ON PROFITS 5p

DIVIDENDS 2p

DEVELOPMENT 5p

M & S is an international company with stores in Europe and Canada and we export to many others throughout the world.

In Canada we have 178 stores, 56 called Marks & Spencer which sell only St Michael goods mostly made in Canada. The others, although owned by our Canadian company have different names and don't sell St Michael.

In Europe we have four stores, two in Paris, one in Brussels and one in Lyon. They all sell St Michael textiles and foods from the ranges available in the UK. Dublin will make a fifth European store when it opens in November.

The Marks & Spencer Group sales, inclusive of VAT and Sales Taxes, were as follows:

SALES BY U.K. STORES	£1431.7m
SALES BY EUROPEAN STORES	£27.4m
SALES BY CANADIAN STORES	£65.5m
EXPORTS	£25.5m
GROUP TOTAL	£1550.1m

HOW WE DID AS A GROUP

Appendix 3 Discount Tables

Present value of 1 at compound interest: $(1 + r)^{-n}$

YEARS (n)   INTEREST RATES (r)

n	1	2	3	4	5	6	7	8	9	10	11	12	13	14	15	16	17	18	19	20
1	0.9901	0.9804	0.9709	0.9615	0.9524	0.9434	0.9346	0.9259	0.9174	0.9091	0.9009	0.8929	0.8850	0.8772	0.8696	0.8621	0.8547	0.8475	0.8403	0.8333
2	0.9803	0.9612	0.9426	0.9246	0.9070	0.8900	0.8734	0.8573	0.8417	0.8264	0.8116	0.7972	0.7831	0.7695	0.7561	0.7432	0.7305	0.7182	0.7062	0.6944
3	0.9706	0.9423	0.9151	0.8890	0.8638	0.8396	0.8163	0.7938	0.7722	0.7513	0.7312	0.7118	0.6931	0.6750	0.6575	0.6407	0.6244	0.6086	0.5934	0.5787
4	0.9610	0.9238	0.8885	0.8548	0.8227	0.7921	0.7629	0.7350	0.7084	0.6830	0.6587	0.6355	0.6133	0.5921	0.5718	0.5523	0.5337	0.5158	0.4987	0.4823
5	0.9515	0.9057	0.8626	0.8219	0.7835	0.7473	0.7130	0.6806	0.6499	0.6209	0.5935	0.5674	0.5428	0.5194	0.4972	0.4761	0.4561	0.4371	0.4190	0.4019
6	0.9420	0.8880	0.8375	0.7903	0.7462	0.7050	0.6663	0.6302	0.5963	0.5645	0.5346	0.5066	0.4803	0.4556	0.4323	0.4104	0.3898	0.3704	0.3521	0.3349
7	0.9327	0.8706	0.8131	0.7599	0.7107	0.6651	0.6227	0.5835	0.5470	0.5132	0.4817	0.4523	0.4251	0.3996	0.3759	0.3538	0.3332	0.3139	0.2959	0.2791
8	0.9235	0.8535	0.7894	0.7307	0.6768	0.6274	0.5820	0.5403	0.5019	0.4665	0.4339	0.4039	0.3762	0.3506	0.3269	0.3050	0.2848	0.2660	0.2487	0.2326
9	0.9143	0.8368	0.7664	0.7026	0.6446	0.5919	0.5439	0.5002	0.4604	0.4241	0.3909	0.3606	0.3329	0.3075	0.2843	0.2630	0.2434	0.2255	0.2090	0.1938
10	0.9053	0.8203	0.7441	0.6756	0.6139	0.5584	0.5083	0.4632	0.4224	0.3855	0.3522	0.3220	0.2946	0.2697	0.2472	0.2267	0.2080	0.1911	0.1756	0.1615
11	0.8963	0.8043	0.7224	0.6496	0.5847	0.5268	0.4751	0.4289	0.3875	0.3505	0.3173	0.2875	0.2607	0.2366	0.2149	0.1954	0.1778	0.1619	0.1476	0.1346
12	0.8874	0.7885	0.7014	0.6246	0.5568	0.4970	0.4440	0.3971	0.3555	0.3186	0.2858	0.2567	0.2307	0.2076	0.1869	0.1685	0.1520	0.1372	0.1240	0.1122
13	0.8787	0.7730	0.6810	0.6006	0.5303	0.4688	0.4150	0.3677	0.3262	0.2897	0.2575	0.2292	0.2042	0.1821	0.1625	0.1452	0.1252	0.1163	0.1042	0.0935
14	0.8700	0.7579	0.6611	0.5775	0.5051	0.4423	0.3878	0.3405	0.2992	0.2633	0.2320	0.2046	0.1807	0.1597	0.1413	0.1252	0.1110	0.0985	0.0876	0.0779
15	0.8613	0.7430	0.6419	0.5553	0.4810	0.4173	0.3624	0.3152	0.2745	0.2394	0.2090	0.1827	0.1599	0.1401	0.1229	0.1079	0.0949	0.0835	0.0736	0.0649
16	0.8528	0.7284	0.6232	0.5339	0.4581	0.3936	0.3387	0.2919	0.2519	0.2176	0.1883	0.1631	0.1415	0.1229	0.1069	0.0930	0.0811	0.0708	0.0618	0.0541
17	0.8444	0.7142	0.6050	0.5134	0.4363	0.3714	0.3166	0.2703	0.2311	0.1978	0.1696	0.1456	0.1252	0.1078	0.0929	0.0802	0.0693	0.0600	0.0520	0.0451
18	0.8360	0.7002	0.5874	0.4936	0.4155	0.3503	0.2959	0.2502	0.2120	0.1799	0.1528	0.1300	0.1108	0.0946	0.0808	0.0691	0.0592	0.0508	0.0437	0.0376
19	0.8277	0.6864	0.5703	0.4746	0.3957	0.3305	0.2765	0.2317	0.1945	0.1635	0.1377	0.1161	0.0981	0.0829	0.0703	0.0596	0.0506	0.0431	0.0367	0.0313
20	0.8195	0.6730	0.5537	0.4564	0.3769	0.3118	0.2584	0.2145	0.1784	0.1486	0.1240	0.1037	0.0868	0.0728	0.0611	0.0514	0.0433	0.0365	0.0308	0.0261
25	0.7795	0.6095	0.4776	0.3751	0.2953	0.2330	0.1842	0.1460	0.1160	0.0923	0.0736	0.0588	0.0471	0.0378	0.0304	0.0245	0.0197	0.0160	0.0129	0.0105
30	0.7419	0.5521	0.4120	0.3083	0.2314	0.1741	0.1314	0.0994	0.0754	0.0573	0.0437	0.0334	0.0256	0.0196	0.0151	0.0116	0.0090	0.0070	0.0054	0.0042
35	0.7059	0.5000	0.3554	0.2534	0.1813	0.1301	0.0937	0.0676	0.0490	0.0356	0.0259	0.0189	0.0139	0.0102	0.0075	0.0055	0.0041	0.0030	0.0023	0.0017
40	0.6717	0.4529	0.3066	0.2083	0.1420	0.0972	0.0668	0.0460	0.0318	0.0221	0.0154	0.0107	0.0075	0.0053	0.0037	0.0026	0.0019	0.0013	0.0010	0.0005
45	0.6391	0.4102	0.2644	0.1712	0.1113	0.0727	0.0476	0.0313	0.0207	0.0137	0.0091	0.0061	0.0041	0.0027	0.0019	0.0013	0.0009	0.0006	0.0004	0.0003
50	0.6080	0.3715	0.2281	0.1407	0.0872	0.0543	0.0339	0.0213	0.0134	0.0085	0.0054	0.0035	0.0022	0.0014	0.0009	0.0006	0.0004	0.0003	0.0002	0.0001

Present value of an annuity of 1: $\dfrac{1-(1+r)^{-n}}{r}$

YEARS (n)   INTEREST RATES (r)

n	1	2	3	4	5	6	7	8	9	10	11	12	13	14	15	16	17	18
1	0.9901	0.9804	0.9709	0.9615	0.9524	0.9434	0.9346	0.9259	0.9174	0.9091	0.9009	0.8929	0.8850	0.8772	0.8696	0.8621	0.8547	0.8475
2	1.9704	1.9416	1.9135	1.8861	1.8594	1.8334	1.8080	1.7833	1.7591	1.7355	1.7125	1.6901	1.6681	1.6467	1.6257	1.6052	1.5852	1.5656
3	2.9410	2.8839	2.8286	2.7751	2.7232	2.6730	2.6243	2.5771	2.5313	2.4869	2.4437	2.4018	2.3612	2.3216	2.2832	2.2459	2.2096	2.1743
4	3.9020	3.8077	3.7171	3.6299	3.5460	3.4651	3.3872	3.3121	3.2397	3.1699	3.1024	3.0373	2.9745	2.9137	2.8550	2.7982	2.7432	2.6901
5	4.8534	4.7135	4.5797	4.4518	4.3295	4.2124	4.1002	3.9927	3.8897	3.7908	3.6959	3.6048	3.5172	3.4331	3.3522	3.2743	3.1993	3.1272
6	5.7955	5.6014	5.4172	5.2421	5.0757	4.9173	4.7665	4.6229	4.4859	4.3553	4.2305	4.1114	3.9975	3.8887	3.7845	3.6847	3.5892	3.4976
7	6.7282	6.4720	6.2303	6.0021	5.7864	5.5824	5.3893	5.2064	5.0330	4.8684	4.7122	4.5638	4.4226	4.2883	4.1604	4.0386	3.9224	3.8115
8	7.6517	7.3255	7.0197	6.7327	6.4632	6.2098	5.9713	5.7466	5.5348	5.3349	5.1461	4.9676	4.7988	4.6389	4.4873	4.3436	4.2072	4.0776
9	8.5660	8.1622	7.7861	7.4353	7.1078	6.8017	6.5152	6.2469	5.9952	5.7590	5.5370	5.3282	5.1317	4.9464	4.7716	4.6065	4.4506	4.3030
10	9.4713	8.9826	8.5302	8.1109	7.7217	7.3601	7.0236	6.7101	6.4177	6.1446	5.8892	5.6502	5.4262	5.2161	5.0188	4.8332	4.6586	4.4941
11	10.3676	9.7868	9.2526	8.7605	8.3064	7.8869	7.4987	7.1390	6.8052	6.4951	6.2065	5.9377	5.6869	5.4527	5.2337	5.0286	4.8364	4.6560
12	11.2551	10.5753	9.9540	9.3851	8.8633	8.3838	7.9427	7.5361	7.1607	6.8137	6.4924	6.1944	5.9176	5.6603	5.4206	5.1971	4.9884	4.7932
13	12.1337	11.3484	10.6350	9.9856	9.3936	8.8527	8.3577	7.9038	7.4869	7.1034	6.7499	6.4235	6.1218	5.8424	5.5831	5.3423	5.1183	4.9095
14	13.0037	12.1062	11.2961	10.5631	9.8986	9.2950	8.7455	8.2442	7.7862	7.3667	6.9819	6.6282	6.3025	6.0021	5.7245	5.4675	5.2293	5.0081
15	13.8651	12.8493	11.9379	11.1184	10.3797	9.7122	9.1079	8.5595	8.0607	7.6061	7.1909	6.8109	6.4624	6.1422	5.8474	5.5755	5.3242	5.0916
16	14.7179	13.5777	12.5611	11.6523	10.8378	10.1059	9.4466	8.8514	8.3126	7.8237	7.3792	6.9740	6.6039	6.2651	5.9542	5.6685	5.4053	5.1624
17	15.5623	14.2919	13.1661	12.1657	11.2741	10.4773	9.7632	9.1216	8.5436	8.0216	7.5488	7.1196	6.7291	6.3729	6.0472	5.7487	5.4746	5.2223
18	16.3983	14.9920	13.7535	12.6593	11.6896	10.8276	10.0591	9.3719	8.7556	8.2014	7.7016	7.2497	6.8399	6.4674	6.1280	5.8178	5.5339	5.2732
19	17.2260	15.6785	14.3238	13.1339	12.0853	11.1581	10.3356	9.6036	8.9501	8.3649	7.8393	7.3658	6.9380	6.5504	6.1982	5.8775	5.5845	5.3162
20	18.0456	16.3514	14.8775	13.5903	12.4622	11.4699	10.5940	9.8181	9.1285	8.5136	7.9633	7.4694	7.0248	6.6231	6.2593	5.9288	5.6278	5.3527
25	22.0232	19.5235	17.4131	15.6221	14.0939	12.7834	11.6536	10.6748	9.8226	9.0770	8.4217	7.8431	7.3300	6.8729	6.4641	6.0971	5.7662	5.4669
30	25.8077	22.3965	19.6004	17.2920	15.3725	13.7648	12.4090	11.2578	10.2737	9.4269	8.6938	8.0552	7.4957	7.0027	6.5660	6.1772	5.8294	5.5168
35	29.4086	24.9986	21.4872	18.6646	16.3742	14.4982	12.9477	11.6546	10.5668	9.6442	8.8552	8.1755	7.5856	7.0700	6.6166	6.2153	5.8582	5.5386
40	32.8347	27.3555	23.1148	19.7928	17.1591	15.0463	13.3317	11.9246	10.7574	9.7791	8.9511	8.2438	7.6344	7.1050	6.6418	6.2335	5.8713	5.5482
45	36.0945	29.4902	24.5187	20.7200	17.7741	15.4558	13.6055	12.1084	10.8812	9.8628	9.0079	8.2825	7.6609	7.1232	6.6543	6.2421	5.8773	5.5523
50	39.1961	31.4236	25.7298	21.4822	18.2559	15.7619	13.8007	12.2335	10.9617	9.9148	9.0417	8.3045	7.6752	7.1327	6.6605	6.2463	5.8801	5.5541

References

CHAPTER 1: INTRODUCTION TO FINANCIAL ACCOUNTING

1. T. A. Lee and D. P. Tweedie, 'Accounting Information: An Investigation of Private Shareholders' Usage', *Accounting and Business Research* (Autumn 1975; Winter 1975).
2. 'Ethical Guide for Members', *Management Accounting* (March 1979).
3. E. Flamholtz, *Human Resource Accounting* (Dickenson Publishing, 1974).
4. A. Rabarts, 'What the Auditor Needs to Know About Fraud', *Accountancy* (December 1978).
   M. Firth, 'Recent Empirical Studies in Auditing', *Accountancy* (February 1979).
5. *The Audit of Public Companies* (LEFTA, 1977).
6. *The Audit Committee Guide* (Second Edition) (Coopers and Lybrand, 1976).

CHAPTER 2: FINANCIAL REPORTING

1. *Accountancy* (April 1978).
2. *City Code on Takeovers and Mergers*, 4th Edition (The City Working Party, 1976).
3. Inflation Accounting: Report of the Inflation Accounting Committee (*Sandilands*). Cmnd 6225 (HMSO, September 1975).
4. *The Corporate Report*, A Discussion Paper (Accounting Standards Steering Committee, 1975).
5. Disclosure of information to trade unions for collective bargaining purposes (*ACAS Code of Practice*) (HMSO, 1977).
6. *The Corporate Report: An Academic View*, Occasional Paper No. 8 (Research Committee of the ICAEW, 1976).

CHAPTER 4: INFLATION ACCOUNTING

1. *Accounting in Relation to Changes in the Purchasing Power of Money* (ICAEW, May 1952).
2. *Accounting for Changes in the Purchasing Power of Money*, ED8 (January 1973).

3. Inflation Accounting: Report of the Inflation Accounting Committee (*Sandilands*), CMND 6225 (HMSO, September 1975).
4. 'Price Index Numbers for Current Cost Accounting', Central Statistical Office (HMSO).
5. Henry Gold, 'SSAP 16 – The End of the Beginning?', *The Accountant's Magazine* (April, 1980).

CHAPTER 5: FINANCIAL PLANNING

1. E. I. Altman, *Corporate Bankruptcy in the United States* (Lexington, 1970); (see also *Journal of Finance*, Vol. XXIII, September 1968).

CHAPTER 6: SOURCES OF BUSINESS FINANCE

1. See, for example, J. R. Franks and J. E. Broyles, *Modern Managerial Finance* (Wiley, 1979); J. M. Samuels and F. M. Wilkes, *Management of Company Finance* (Nelson, 1975) and J. F. Weston and E. F. Brigham, *Essentials of Managerial Finance*, (5th Edition) (Holt Saunders, 1979).

CHAPTER 8: CAPITAL INVESTMENT APPRAISAL

1. E.g. H. Bierman and S. Smidt, *The Capital Budgeting Decision* (Macmillan, 1975); J. T. S. Porterfield, *Investment Decisions and Capital Costs*, (Prentice-Hall, 1965).

CHAPTER 10: CONTRIBUTION ANALYSIS

1. R. H. Parker, *Management Accounting: An Historical Perspective* (Macmillan, 1969).

CHAPTER 11: BUDGETING, BUDGETARY CONTROL AND CORPORATE PLANNING

1. Henri Fayol, *General and Industrial Administration* (Pitman, 1949). (Translated by Constance Storrs from the original Administration Industrielle et Générale, 1916.)
2. C. Argyris, *The Impact of Budgets on People* (Controllership Foundation, 1952).
3. E. H. Caplan, *Management Accounting and Behavioural Science* (Addison-Wesley, 1971).
4. D. McGregor, *The Human Side of Enterprise* (McGraw-Hill, 1960).
5. C. H. Handy, *Understanding Organisations* (Penguin, 1976).
6. A. Wildavsky, 'Policy Analysis is What Information Systems are Not', *Accounting, Organisations and Society*, 3(1) (1978).

Further Reading

CHAPTER 2: FINANCIAL REPORTING

Accounting Principles and Practices in European Countries (Price Waterhouse, 1976).

J. Dearden and J. Shank, *Financial Accounting and Reporting: A Contemporary Emphasis* (Prentice-Hall, 1975).

R. W. Estes, *Corporate Social Accounting* (Wiley, 1975).

T. Gambling, *Societal Accounting* (Allen & Unwin, 1974).

C. Hird, *Your Employer's Profits*, Workers' Handbook No. 2 (Pluto Press, 1975).

How to read a Balance Sheet (Programmed Text) (ILO, 1966).

K. M. Oldham, *Accounting Systems and Practice in Europe* (Gower Press, 1975).

Lee and Lynn Seidler, *Social Accounting: Theory, Issues and Cases* (Melville, 1975).

Survey of Published Accounts, 1978 (ICAEW, 1979).

CHAPTER 3: THE ANALYSIS OF ANNUAL ACCOUNTS

W. T. Baxter, *Depreciation* (Sweet & Maxwell, 1971).

G. Foster, *Financial Statement Analysis* (Prentice-Hall, 1978).

P. R. A. Kirkman, *Modern Credit Management* (Allen & Unwin, 1977).

M. Tamari, *Financial Ratios: Analysis and Prediction* (Paul Elek, 1978).

CHAPTER 4: INFLATION ACCOUNTING

'SSAP 16', *Accountancy* (April, 1980).

A. G. Campbell, 'SSAP 16, A Practical Guide', *The Accountant's Magazine* (April and May 1980).

CHAPTER 5: FINANCIAL PLANNING

E. I. Altman and A. W. Sametz (eds), *Financial Crisis: Institutions and Markets in a Fragile Environment* (Wiley, 1977).

J. Argenti, *Corporate Collapse* (McGraw-Hill, 1976).

D. E. Vaughn, Norgaard and Bennett, *Financial Planning and Management: A Budgetary Approach* (Goodyear Publishing, 1972).

CHAPTER 6: SOURCES OF BUSINESS FINANCE

C. Aydon, *Financing Your Company* (Management Publications, 1972).
Committee to Review the Functioning of Financial Institutions, (Chairman: Sir H. Wilson) (HMSO, 1977/8).

CHAPTER 7: THE STOCK EXCHANGE

J. H. Dunning and E. V. Morgan (eds), *An Economic Study of the City of London* (Allen & Unwin, 1971).
H. McRae and F. Cairncross, *Capital City* (Eyre Methuen, 1973).

CHAPTER 9: INTRODUCTION TO MANAGEMENT ACCOUNTING

R. N. Anthony and J. S. Reece, *Management Accounting: Text and Cases* (Irwin, 1975).
C. T. Horngren, *Cost Accounting: A Managerial Emphasis* (Prentice-Hall, 1972).
C. T. Horngren, *Accounting for Management Control: An Introduction* (Prentice-Hall, 1974).

CHAPTER 10: CONTRIBUTION ANALYSIS

B. Taylor and G. Wills (eds), *Pricing Strategy* (Staples, 1969).

CHAPTER 11: BUDGETING, BUDGETARY CONTROL AND CORPORATE PLANNING

Budgeting: H. C. Edey, *Business Budgets and Accounts* (Hutchinson, 1966); G. H. Hofstede, *The Game of Budget Control* (Tavistock, 1972).
Corporate Planning: H. I. Ansoff, *Strategic Management* (Macmillan, 1979); J. Argenti, *Systematic Corporate Planning* (Nelson, 1974); B. Taylor, article in *Long Range Planning* (December 1976).
Marketing and Marketing Research: M. J. Baker, *Marketing: An Introductory Text* (Macmillan, 1979); P. Chisnall, *Marketing Research* (McGraw-Hill, 1973); P. Kotler, *Marketing Management: Analysis, Planning and Control* (Prentice-Hall, 1976); A. Wilson, *The Assessment of Industrial Markets* (Hutchinson, 1968).
Organisational Behaviour: C. Handy, *Understanding Organisations* (Penguin, 1976); J. W. Hunt, *Managing People at Work: A Manager's Guide to Behaviour in Organisations* (McGraw-Hill, 1979).

APPENDIX 2: VALUE ADDED STATEMENTS

G. Smith, *Wealth Creation – The Added Value Concept* (Institute of Practitioners in Work Study, Organisation and Methods, 1973).
E. G. Wood, 'How to Add Value', *Management Today* (May, 1974).
E. G. Wood, *Added Value – The Key to Prosperity* (Anchor Press, 1978).

Index

206